P9-CEG-083

TABLE OF CONTENTS

EVOLUTIONARY WORK

*Unleashing Your Potential
in Extraordinary Times*

by Patricia DiVecchio

PEARHOUSE
PRESS

Published by Pearhouse Press, Inc., Pittsburgh, PA 15208
www.pearhousepress.com

First Printing: June 2010

Printed in the United States of America

Library of Congress Control Number: 2009937190

ISBN: 978-0-9802355-4-8

Cover and Book Design: Mike Murray
Cover Background Artwork: Douglas G. Nelson
Author Headshot: Betty Morales from B. Morales Photography

EVOLUTIONARY WORK

*Unleashing Your Potential
in Extraordinary Times*

To my parents, whose life was a different adventure than mine but an adventure still. You taught me to be my own person, and I'm sure you're so proud.

INTRODUCTION

A. The Times Couldn't Be Better

*"Everyone has talent. What is rare is the courage to follow
the talent to the dark place where it leads. "*
– Erica Jong

It seems like a contradiction in terms. The times, in many ways,
seem like the worst in a lifetime. We are experiencing unparalleled
change on planet Earth, from global warming to financial upheaval to
the breakdown of work and business as we know it. Our vulnerability,
humanity and sense of security are being tested. Who we are as a
human race, along with the institutional structures and life-long beliefs
held so dear, are being redefined right before our eyes.

No one is immune. At some level we are all being affected. When
hard times come, as now, we tend to pull back and contract. We think
hunkering down while still being committed to work as usual is the
route to take when, in actuality, the opposite is true. Reinvention from
the inside out is needed, an overhaul that results in a new enlightened
model of work and business.

We are all being asked to evolve at what feels like the speed of
light. The pain is now too great for us to stay complacent. Regardless
of where you find yourself—without a job, underemployed or just
keeping your business afloat—there is a lot to learn and to change.

In some cases the lessons are apparent and in others they fall under
"we don't know that we don't know," which makes them very difficult

indeed. In all cases the lessons are in the duality of simple and complex but yet are basic to human nature. The problem is we haven't been living or working true to our nature for a long time.

Repeating the past is not the answer. Insanity has been defined as doing the same thing over and over again expecting to achieve new results. So are we insane or just creatures of habit? A bit of both, perhaps. It's not easy to shed old skin when it's the only coat you've ever worn, even when you know it's for the best.

[The following is the first of many personal responses that I will be writing to share my own experiences. Hopefully, these reflections will encourage you to do the same, digging deep within yourself to uncover your truth and your greater work.]

> *Personally I drift in and out of feeling out of control and knowing I'm evolving into a truer sense of self and work. When feeling out of control, I'm afraid everything I've built up over the years of my business is tumbling down. Is this ego or paranoia? Could be either or both, I suppose. When feeling on the right path and open to learning the lessons put in front of me, I'm able to step back and reevaluate my approach to business to meet the needs of today; I'm more true to my heart's longing; and I'm creating the business community I long for. I'm in this boat with you. Always the first student of my own work.*

So what is the best next step, as individuals and business owners? How do we tap and leverage human potential, humanity and wisdom first within ourselves and then through our work/business? How do we create new business models that meet the deeper human needs of our global economy?

We start by asking a new set of questions. Tough questions. They are deep, challenging and heartfelt. The time to face them couldn't be better.

Here are some of those questions. Are you ready to answer them?

1. Opportunities are knocking on the door – Are you stepping up to your next level of both personal and business growth? If not, why not?
2. We are all very wise – Are you leveraging your unique wisdom both within your work and for the greater good of us all?
3. Greater risks are being called for – Is the outdated work security blanket stopping you from making the changes you know are needed?
4. Have you stepped back from the financial upheaval to realize the lessons learned and made appropriate long-term changes, or are you just breathing a sigh of relief, believing the worst is behind you, and carrying on with the status quo?

These economic times are forcing everyone to work differently. Radical, not simple, change is needed. We have the world of work all backwards in so many ways. Work and business is not an external event but an internal perspective that generates itself in the marketplace. Those taking the high road are the ones who will succeed. Individuals who will ultimately survive and thrive are the ones willing to adopt a more enlightened mental work model—where making a difference and seeing a good return are equal priorities.

If you are ready for a quantum leap, this book is for you. If you want a quick fix, then you'll have to look elsewhere. Once the willingness is there to take this challenge, we have the option of doing something about it—or burying it even deeper.

Take the first step, risk more than ever before and don't stop. The actions and answers may not all be apparent, and you may not be sure where to start, but the time is now. You have the power to influence reality—to create the work world of your choice. *Your* work is worth the effort.

> *"You never change things by fighting the existing reality. To change something, build a new model that makes the existing model obsolete. "*
> – *Buckminster Fuller*

3

B. Work as an Evolutionary Path

Work and business are not what we think. They're not ways to make a living or a name for ourselves. This definition served an antiquated notion of business, a model based on control over others and profit at the expense of good will. These are new times. A new consciousness is asking us to be more responsible for ourselves, the work we do and the planet we live on. In return we have an opportunity to create the future of choice, a future that will yield life and work beyond what we can now imagine.

Newly defined, work and business are forums for personal and professional evolution. They are a means to self-actualization and beyond. Now is a time for transcendence, when we can help others self-actualize.

Work is not an outer-referencing of what the marketplace will bear, but an inner-referencing of our unique purpose, molded and packaged for the marketplace to buy. I've never encountered someone with a purpose that was not dearly needed in the world.

Matthew Fox, in his *Reinvention of Work – A New Vision of Livelihood for Our Time,* states, "In our time, we are being called to reexamine our work: how we do it; whom it is helping or hurting; what it is we do; and what we might be doing if we were to let go of our present work and follow a deeper call."

Past industrial and technological revolutions have provided tools to do work differently. It's our turn to provide the consciousness. This evolution is happening from the ground up, where the view of money, power and productivity are seen in a new light. Purposeful work encourages the blossoming of spirit, the healing needed and ultimately the expression of who we are.

Work is no longer about jobs, unemployment or retirement. If work is actually about innate purpose, then how can we retire from our very selves? The traditional work/business structure keeps us chained to an unhealthy reality that hardly cultivates the soul. We believe we are employed by a system, a boss, an organization, when the truth is we are employed by a power much higher than any of these.

Jeremy Rifkin, in *The End of Work*, talks about the demise of the job in a traditional sense. I would ask if this is a catastrophe or an opportunity. This may well be a blessing in disguise. The demise of the old model of work is actually granting us freedom to explore our greater selves, to build internal strength and to be responsible for our own learning and our destiny. We can no longer control or be controlled by the traditional job structure. We are too self-aware, conscious, educated and heart-centered to allow this false sense of life and work to continue.

If we are willing to surrender to a higher calling, then our work will be presented on a silver platter. But do be aware that this journey is only for the strong of heart. Much will be asked of us. In turn, much will be given. We will be tested every step of the way, for strength is essential. Surrendering to a purposeful course is necessary for the evolution of the universe. Some are realizing this and acting on it—others are coming along kicking and screaming. The choice is ours. I always say give it a chance. It can't hurt, and it might help.

We all have unique work to do. But what does that look like? How and where do we start? With willingness and desire. You wouldn't be reading this book if you didn't have both. We are here, together, to help you in this process.

The human race is evolving at a blinding pace moving beyond Abraham Maslow's original hierarchy *(see next page)* used to illustrate how human beings are motivated by unsatisfied needs. We move up and down this ladder depending on many aspects of life and work such as our mind-set and circumstances. The satisfaction of these needs is core to our advancement and evolution.

The areas below, in parentheses, have subsequently been added to Maslow's original hierarchy.

(Beyond) Maslow's Hierarchy of Needs

+ **(Transcendence – to ultimately help others to self-actualize)**
+ **Self-Actualization – to become everything one is capable of becoming**
+ **(Aesthetic Needs – for beauty, balance and form)**
+ **(Cognitive Needs – for knowledge, meaning and self-awareness)**
+ **Self-Esteem Needs – for achievement, status, responsibility and reputation**
+ **Love and Belonging Needs – to feel acceptance and to love and be loved**
+ **Safety Needs – for security, safety and a predictable orderly world**
+ **Biological and Physiological Needs – basic human needs for such things as air, water, food, sleep, etc.**

Adapted by persons unknown based on Maslow's *Hierarchy of Needs*

Where are you on this continuum? Are you stuck in fear-based security or grounded in seeking self-actualization? This book and process will guide you up the ladder.

C. Book Overview

Evolutionary Work is an opportunity, a challenge and a call to action. It's not a passive read or a conversation piece. If you're willing, it will provide a new view of your self, your work and your business choices, as well as ways to overcome the internal obstacles to your success.

The book is based on **Seven Evolutionary Tools** we already have within us that we either aren't aware of, haven't fully developed or haven't wanted to face. Developing them demands a high degree of responsibility, and the power to do this is not freely given. I've developed and fine-tuned these Tools over the last 15 years. Hundreds of brave individuals have been part of the process, and you are now among them.

If you stick to this process, your results are guaranteed. Upon completion, my hope is for you to:

✦ *Know yourself better than ever, enabling confidence, courage, new ideas and new work/business opportunities.*

✦ *Realize that we are the ones that stop ourselves from creating work that is more meaningful. We are the solution, hope and possibility.*

✦ *Have a clearer and greater sense of your work that meets a deeper need in the marketplace.*

✦ *Benefit others from your modeling of healthy, enlightened ways to live and work.*

✦ *Package your work purpose as viable and sustainable in the market-place.*

✦ *Be a force to be reckoned with. The world will gain from the ripple effect of all you say and do. You will be playing much larger and bolder.*

Thanks for joining the evolution.

Sincerely,
Patricia

D. Overview of the Seven Evolutionary Tools

Each Tool is a self-contained unit and a part of a greater whole. Proceed through the Tools as given. The goal is to build a new awareness, foundation and work future, one day at a time.

Tool 1: Reinventing Your Work/Business

a. *You are more than you imagine*

b. *Evolving beyond old patterns*

c. *Maturing takes forgiveness*

d. *Predicting your future*

Learn how often our beliefs around self, work and business are based on a set of limiting, negative, outdated and even false assumptions. These backward beliefs have kept us playing small. Here is an opportunity to expose, heal and evolve our sense of self into a new world of work.

Tool 2: No Competition

a. *They really did break the mold*

b. *Tools for uncovering your unique work/business composite*

c. *Mind-mapping new work/business opportunities*

No two of us are alike, nor will we ever be. When doing our true work, there is no one to compete against except ourselves. This Tool engages all of who we are—a unique composite of innate skills and talents, dreams and desires, experience and education. With a focus on natural abilities and gifts, we will build a new, value-based perspective of who we are and the work/business we are meant to do.

Tool 3: Creating a Strong Foundation

a. *No doubt about it*

b. *Stop fooling ourselves — work ≠ security*

c. *New tools = new foundation = new work*

d. *Beyond self-deception to self-realization*

We will need the strength of the gods to live and work beyond the norm. Naysayers, well-intentioned friends and our own deep-seated fears will show their face. The focus here is to develop a new strength of "nothing to lose and a lot to gain." A solid inner foundation is our end goal. If we don't learn to lead with confidence and courage, then we lead with self-deception and self-doubt.

Tool 4: Fear as an Ally

a. *Worst enemy/best friend*

b. *Don't fear what you want most*

c. *Embracing your resistance*

d. *Fear is love in disguise*

Having gained self-responsibility we can now recognize our part. Now is the time to act, not to be afraid. If you can stand firm to your vision of new work, fear will be on your side—a motivator in disguise. This Tool is an opportunity to embrace those fears and enlist them for the greater good. Fear can lead us to the solution.

Tool 5: Wisdom as the Next Evolutionary Leap

a. *Your intellect is passé*

b. *Trusting yourself to tell the truth*

c. *It is our work to be wise*

d. *Defining & developing wisdom*

e. *The Wisdom-Centered Visionary*™

A new level of thinking alone is not going to generate the answers we need. A new level of *being* is the only answer. Here we learn to cultivate new answers through the collective use of our heart, wisdom and body, along with universal knowledge. Einstein said, "We can't get new answers to problems from the same level of thinking that the answers were created from in the first place." This Tool takes you beyond just new thinking to new being in order to learn how to become a visionary like no other—a Wisdom-Centered Visionary™.

Tool 6: A Critical Time for Work/Business Evolution

a. *Work as an expression of love*

b. *Decision making from middle ground*

c. *Transforming your mental frame of reference*

d. *Evolving into the "frame" of purposeful work*

Being a part of the new work/business evolution requires an entirely different presence in the world. Creating new work realities that encourage both individual and business evolution will ask much of us. The mental model we hold about ourselves and work in general is all backwards. In this tool, we are asked to take a quantum step if we are to live the life we are meant to live. The step will require us to evolve into a new enlightened frame of reference.

Tool 7: Purposeful Work – Thriving in the Marketplace

a. *Solidifying your purpose, vision & mission*

b. *Meeting deeper needs in the marketplace*

c. *Building relationships – attracting the right audience*

d. *Strategically creating from the future*

Now is the time for everything to come together. The insights, internal shifts, enlightened awarenesses and so much more. You are, without a doubt, at the point of no return. Here you will read about the stories of others and how they evolved their innate purpose to thriving work/businesses. May you learn from both their hard lessons and their successes. It is time to bring concrete form to your work and match it to the marketplace. Ultimately, being and modeling your new work model will attract the largest audience.

Appendix: Being a Part of the New Work/Business Evolution

a. *You are the future*

b. *Success is a collective effort – supporting each other*

c. *It's time to celebrate*

Work/business is meant to be an incubator of the human spirit—as is all of life. We all have an ongoing role in this transformative process. It is our commitment to this enlightened perspective that will heal us and those we work with. The appendix focuses on joining together to support and celebrate each other. We have greatness in us and all around us. Work well done!

E. Making the Best Use of This Book

*"Faith is trusting, when you come
to the edge of everything you know,
that you will either step off on to solid ground,
or be taught how to fly."*
– Anonymous

This process is different for everyone. It's a time to create what might seem like the impossible and to dream BIG. The following three steps will prepare you for this journey.

EVOLUTIONARY WORK CASE STUDY

CYNTHIA

Coaching & Purposeful Business Tele-Circles

I first met Patricia during a time I'd designated for manifesting of my dreams, leaving some of the security of full time and some private practice. Her initial coaching included visualizing the completion of some long-held projects into a small visual "note."

Over the last 5 years, I've had the privilege of working with Patricia to manifest the husband, home and much of the work of my inner desires. My time in circular unproductive thinking (once a mainstay of life) is now much less. The foundations for my life work have gained footing with her encouragement and tutelage. I find this process of working with her newest book in group format has helped me identify and loosen some of the old neural networks that prevent success. I love the way her powerful questions can open new doors!

Recently I embarked on learning Integrative Health Coaching. I feel indebted to Patricia for having asked powerful questions and for giving me the opportunity to offer them to others. I realize I've also had some great coaching on how to coach others!

We are collectively shifting work/business out of the past and into the future, and your commitment is part of the process. Because this process takes time, we want to honor your effort up front. We recommend a minimum of 20 minutes a day to focus on this process. If possible, make this a morning ritual, when you are fresh and clear of mind.

First: **Adopt the mindset and guidelines that follow**.

This will help create fertile ground for the important work to happen. Keep these in the forefront of your mind as you continue.

1. *Challenge your assumptions about yourself, your work and your business.*

   You are more than you think you are. So is your work or business! All thinking is limited, based on our sole perspective. Learn to question your thinking, not as wrong, but as possibly outdated. Only enlightened thinking will create the new mental model of work.

2. *Suspend judgment and create curiosity.*

   Judgment prevents forward movement. It puts up a wall so high that nothing new or different is given a second thought. Curiosity, on the other hand, creates wonderment, excitement and action. The more curious and open-minded you are, the more successful you will be.

3. *Develop time for reflection.*

   New answers surface as you step back to be the objective observer. It's looking from the outside in, with yourself and your work as the subject. Silence is hard to come by, but it's essential. Please give yourself the time.

4. *Let your emotions surface.*

   This process, because of its internal nature, will surface many feelings that have been suppressed over many years of working in dysfunctional work settings. Reflect on them, learn from them, and they will teach you much.

5. *Your success is our success.*

You are not alone in this process. This is a worldwide phenomenon of work/business transformation. If you do this work with others in mind, the end result will be a greater whole. As you give support, you also gain. Know that we are here to support you.

6. *Work from the present with an eye toward the future.*

Our goal is to create the future work/business world of choice—individually and collectively. Envision it and act as if it were now, in the present moment. Enjoy that moment, sense what it feels like, and the future will happen. Honor yourself every step of the way.

7. *Trust that your work purpose is meant to feed your wallet as well as your soul.*

Your purpose is sorely needed in the marketplace. It's up to you to see that this need is met. Your work purpose, over time, will be a viable entity in the new world economy.

8. *Change the way you change.*

This guideline is an expansion of #1. We need to pause between our automatic reactions to situations long enough to enable fresh thinking and, in turn, generate new outcomes. Not easy to do, for we are very hard-wired based on our past. We need to always be "consciously conscious" as we make new choices.

<u>Second</u>: Do the following to integrate the information you learn.

1. *Keep a journal or notebook.*

This journal is the scripting of your new work/business. It's putting your dreams and insights to paper, the first step. As you proceed, clues and patterns will surface. Write them down. At first they may not make sense, but keep at it and let the magic happen. Don't overanalyze. Write what surfaces, and let yourself be surprised. Also use your journal to respond to the Challenges posed throughout the book.

2. *Do the Challenges.*

Complete the Challenges and exercises throughout the book. Realize that your ego has a stake in staying the same and will fight you along the way. Don't let it hold you back. Do one section and exercise daily and be the winner. New work will be yours—guaranteed.

3. *Complete the Purpose Questionnaire.*

On the next page is a pre-evaluation to complete to determine how you currently see yourself as operating from the past or the future. Upon finishing the book, you will be asked to take the Questionnaire again to evaluate your progress—which I'm sure will be excellent.

4. *Questions to get you started.*

Take a few minutes to answer the following questions as specifically and concretely as possible. Set your intention to succeed. Grab your journal and get started.

1. *Why did you choose this book?*
2. *Now that you've come this far, what is motivating you to keep going?*
3. *If your work or business could be anything, what would it be?*
4. *What is the hardest thing you need to face concerning your work/business?*
5. *What would you like to have happen as a result of reading this book? Be specific. Write these as if they were goals.*

Take the one goal, from #5 above, that is the foundation, the major goal upon which everything else will be based, and write it in big letters where you will see it—in front of your face. Read this goal often. See it happening now. You will also be asked to write this in the Purpose Agreement as referenced below.

5. *Complete the Purpose Agreement.*

The more you are committed to yourself and your work/business, the more you will be committed to this process. The greatness of the result is based on this commitment; therefore, take the next step and complete the Purpose Agreement on page 18.

Take the Purpose Questionnaire!

Circle the number that most closely represents you and your work. Check your total score below to see if YOU are a 21ˢᵗ century worker and thinker: self-aware, internally referenced, proactive, and responsible to the greater good of the world.

	Most Often	Half The Time	Rarely
1. I think & act from the future of choice—not the past.	3	2	1
2. I know & leverage my unique skills & talents in the marketplace.	3	2	1
3. I act & work from a sense of greater good.	3	2	1
4. I am self-confident, self-responsible & self-managed.	3	2	1
5. I am a lifelong learner, always growing.	3	2	1
6. I'm passionate about my work purpose.	3	2	1
7. I am entrepreneurial in nature & act on new ideas.	3	2	1
8. I'm acting on "changing the way I change."	3	2	1
9. I work well in chaos & the unknown.	3	2	1
10. I'm a risk-taker, not resigned to 'business as usual.'	3	2	1
11. I see the future as bright with numerous possibilities.	3	2	1
12. I am at peace with myself & my work.	3	2	1

If You Scored 12-21...	If You Scored 22-27...	If You Scored 28-36...
This book is for you. Take the time necessary, and you will gain a renewed sense of self.	*You are straddling the fence between the past and the future. This process will ground you in the present.*	*You're a 21ˢᵗ Century worker and thinker. You are creating a new, enlightened way to work. This process will expand your effort.*

Third: Gathering supplies for the journey

Think of this process as a daily adventure full of excitement and discovery. Like all adventures, it requires preparation and work. You will need to provide yourself with certain supplies. You already have your journal, so why not also, for fun, take along:

a. *Colored pencils and erasers for the playful, creative side of you*

b. *A pad of large drawing paper for creative exercises*

c. *Music to inspire and soothe the soul*

d. *A candle or two to light the way*

e. *A box of tissues for those teary-eyed times*

f. *Other inspirational books to bring you comfort (see Bibliography for suggestions)*

Last but not least—let us support you further:

Go to our web site at www.internationalpurpose.com to learn about the following ways we can support you.

1. The International Purpose free monthly email newsletter. "The Evolution of WORK!" Is written for anyone evolving into more purposeful work—be it a business or an individual. The goal of this newsletter is to provide insight, encouragement and suggestions to all. You can subscribe by logging onto our web site.

2. Join us on Facebook and LinkedIn®.

3. Our Virtual Book Workshop is facilitated over the phone/on-line. It will provide you with a forum to interact with other readers and myself, to ask questions, as well as to receive encouragement and support as you work through the Seven Evolutionary Tools. See the web site for dates/times and investment.

Purpose Agreement

Complete this Purpose Agreement as a joint commitment between you and me, for we are in this together every step of the way. As a dear friend of mine always tells me, "Your success is my success." And so it is for you. Upon completion, please share your major goal with us by emailing office@internationalpurpose.com. We will post, honor and energetically hold your agreement as our joint commitment to your new work future.

This agreement is set this date, _____, between

Patricia DiVecchio and _____(YOUR NAME).

I, _____, agree to give of my whole self in this process, to focus on the greater good, to face my fears, to be courageous unlike ever before and to believe in the creation of what might appear to be the impossible: My work purpose as viable and sustainable in the world economy. I agree to at least a 20-minute/day commitment of time, effort and energy to this evolutionary process. This work happens over time, so I know this is part of a lifelong pursuit. I will do the Challenges and record awarenesses, clues and patterns in my journal. I realize that I am responsible for creating my work purpose and am willing to go through the process required to develop work/business that feeds my wallet as well as my soul. The following goal is the one on which all other goals stand. I am committed to working toward this goal using my head and heart, for that is when the best decision is made.

This is my major goal:

_____

_____

_____

4. You can become a member of a Purposeful Business Tele-Circle. These sessions are tailored to entrepreneurs and small business owners wanting to excel to the next level of their business by utilizing the Seven Evolutionary Tools. We meet by phone/on-line. Go to our web site for dates/times and investment.

The Journey

The journey now is to face your true self. It is time to confront your deep-seated fears, as well as to recognize your greatest potential and humanity. All you have to do is get started, and the journey will gather momentum. Remember, you have nothing to lose, and we all have so much to gain. We await your coming!

"I gift you with the courage to be, to know deeply
the divine design of your life. I gift you with
passion for the possible and the willingness
to bring this possibility into time.
You are more than you think you are, and something
inside you knows it. All the hurts and failures, all the
wanderings, losings, dyings and forgettings were
but part of the gaining of the rich material of your life.
By being wounded, you became vulnerable and available;
by being lost, you were able to be found; by dying,
you learned the power of new birth; by forgetting,
you gained the joy of remembering.
Now I call all parts of you back, a mighty crew, seaworthy
and well-stocked, to set sail for new continents of spirit,
shores of incredible lands where the fractal waves
of many people and many times arrive at last,
and you know that you have gained your birthright.
Welcome home, god and goddess, no longer in hiding."

– Jean Huston

TOOL 1

REINVENTING YOUR WORK / BUSINESS

A. *You Are More Than You Imagine*

B. *Evolving Beyond Old Patterns*

C. *Maturing Takes Forgiveness*

D. *Predicting Your Future*

A. You Are More Than You Imagine

*"Welcome to the first time in the history of the planet
when you truly can choose what you want to be, what you
want to do, what you want to know and where you want
to go... Life has never been easier, and because it has
never been easier, life has never been more hard."*
    *– "Visionary's Handbook: Nine Paradoxes That
    Will Shape the Future of Your Business,"
    Watts Wacker and Jim Taylor*

Take a minute to imagine being all you could be: doing your work or running a business that is better than you ever thought possible. You have no doubt that you are doing your life's work/business. You're leveraging your potential, feeling confident and self-assured and, by the way, thriving in the marketplace. You love your life and your work. There is flow and balance. You truly feel you are making a difference in the world while reaping financial rewards. The people you work with honor who you are and what you do, value your unique skills, validate your ideas, and together you create an environment where everyone learns and grows—personally and professionally.

✦ *Who are you "being"?*
✦ *What are you doing?*
✦ *How are you feeling?*
✦ *Are you living and working without doubt?*

Just imagine! We are all of this and more. We are who we believe ourselves to be. We have within us more power and potential than we can image.

But believing in ourselves is often not something we have learned to do. Have you ever been told you were great, precious and one of a kind? Maybe you were told the opposite: that you shouldn't think too highly of yourself, that you're selfish or different.

So we maintain the status quo, don't rock the boat and stay mum. In doing this we stifle our work potential and make excuses not to act. We play along with the current situation and hold onto what we have—limited as it might be. We follow the negative patterns dictating life, deadening ourselves just a little bit more each day.

We ask ourselves:

✦ *Who am I to think so highly of myself?*

✦ *What do I have to offer that is so unique?*

✦ *Even if I knew my potential, could I live up to it?*

✦ *Could I handle the responsibility it might bring?*

✦ *Do I dare even try?*

So we stay stagnant, uncomfortable but safe—or so we think. For if we choose to imagine and act on this power, this potential, everything will feel like it's coming unglued. Life will change, our current work may seem meaningless and our identity will be challenged. As we see the truth of ourselves, something inside knows it can no longer be ignored. We can no longer keep up the façade—the mask will evaporate. You will be left with only two choices: act or hide.

Those who choose to hide may think they can go back to how it was: living on autopilot, going through the paces. But there is never really a turning back. Once we see the truth of our potential, we know too much—about ourselves, that is. The inner fire has been lit. It may at times weaken and smolder, but it won't go out. We will long for something better. This longing will keep nudging, creating its own type of pain. Life and work, in the old frame, will become uncomfortable and unsatisfactory. If we choose to stay the same, there is now a price to pay. If we choose to hide, we will have given up.

Glimpsing our potential is where desire starts. We all long to be in that place of bliss knowing we are doing greater work. We want to feel the peace and joy that comes with the knowledge of a job well done.

The minute we choose the journey, the journey begins. On some level, we've been waiting a long time for this. Potential has knocked time and again, seeking its rightful place. Its desire for expression

23

can no longer be silenced. The dance has begun, and we have become partners with our purpose.

In 1986 I hit the wall in both my life and work—nothing felt right. The answer to my dilemma was not just any old change—it wasn't about another job, a new boyfriend or a new place to live. These were old escape tactics I knew no longer worked. This was about my soul, my life path. It was time for a new and different journey that would take me to the unknown terrain called me. So I surrendered! That's one of the hardest things to do for someone whose pattern is control at any cost. But I had no choice. Turning back would be like slowly dying on the vine. I read every book I could get my hands on about personal and spiritual growth, attended workshops from the East Coast to the West, participated in a variety of spiritual practices and saw a whole new side of myself. I realized I was not who I thought I was. I was much more!

Now it's your turn, your time and your journey. Have you hit your "wall"? Is the pain great enough to encourage the changes needed? Are you at a point of no return where forward momentum is the only choice? Then come along. Evolution is your destiny.

"Whenever we attempt something difficult there is always a sense that we have to wake some giant slumbering inside ourselves, some greater force as yet hidden from us. We look for better work by first looking for a better image of ourselves. We stir this inner giant to life in order to find the strength to live out life we want from ourselves. We want to live that image not for abstract heroic reasons but because we are desperate for more presence, more responsiveness, more alertness in our work. But first we must be able to recognize the image."

– "Crossing the Unknown Sea: Work as a Pilgrimage of Identity," David Whyte

A. You Are More Than You Imagine – Here's the <u>Challenge</u>:

This is the first of many Challenges meant to have YOU stop, reflect on what matters and put pen to paper. This is where the real work happens. You might hesitate, but don't skip over this Challenge. Give yourself at least 20 minutes. If your responses don't surface, come back later. Finish this exercise before moving forward. Remember to use your journal.

Thank you so much,
Patricia

1. Close your eyes, put a smile on your face and imagine a more self-assured YOU. What do you see yourself doing? How do you feel when you are self-assured, knowing that your work or business is what you want it to be? Give as much detail as possible.

2. The more you get to know and understand yourself, the more clearly defined your work becomes. If you believe this statement is true, what does it mean?

B. Evolving Beyond Old Patterns

We all have an image of self based on a set of assumptions developed over time. This image is often contrived from a series of ideas and ideals based on a limited and limiting set of beliefs. We see ourselves the way our parents, peers and society see us, a frame of reference that does not encompass the full picture.

We've developed ourselves from what we know, not from what could be. We reach to the past to reshape and reshift, saying things will be different. "This new job will be better—it must be; having a new boss will make all the difference" or "The only answer to my success is starting my own business; if only our business could beat out the competition."

Don't rewrite the past, reinvent the future. The limited thinking, fear and separation rooted in our traditional belief system taint any effort to create new work/business. They stifle us with a false sense of security.

I know this well, having lived and worked in Corporate America for years. I played the part, and I was good at it. I was rewarded with money and praise. I was stuck!

It took a deep depression for me to begin to wake up. I began to realize that the life I was leading was actually not mine. It was what I thought I needed to be doing in the world: making money, looking good and being "successful." I was living from a false sense of self. My life was based on the shoulds, oughts and musts, not my dreams and desires.

Of course I saw none of this at the time. I was living and working on autopilot. It's like turning yourself on in the morning and turning off at night—a pretty dismal way to live. This treadmill kept me stuck in my old patterns, reinforcing them every step of the way. That left little room for my essence to develop, let alone flourish.

Old habits die hard. The ways of the past are so ingrained that, until we consciously choose to change outdated beliefs and attitudes, they control our destiny, dictating our thoughts, actions, life and work.

Stopping this cycle begins with stepping back and identifying our core beliefs about self and work/business. This process takes time, requiring tremendous self-awareness and self-acceptance. This is the underpinning for the entire process. If not addressed, the true depth of our purpose and height of our potential will never be reached.

Old beliefs haunt me still. They are so very familiar. I've been thinking these thoughts forever. When they surface, they result in behaviors I'd rather not show the world, behaviors that sabotage my life and my work/business. They play out in many different ways. Sometimes I catch them; sometimes I don't. I often don't realize the damage they've done until someone brings it to my attention. At other times I recognize their presence, but it's too late and I'm having to make amends. If I'm lucky, I catch them before the old belief permeates my thinking, and I feel saved—for the time being.

I wonder if I'll ever be "consciously conscious" enough where not thinking the negative thoughts will be an option. Managing the thoughts is really all I'm after.

Here are some of the old beliefs that I know so well:

1. Patricia, stay close to home.

2. You are no better than anyone else.

3. You can't trust anyone.

4. Patricia, why bother because you aren't going to finish that anyway.

5. You are only valued when you have a good job and make good money.

6. This is just the way life is—you can't change it.

Odd as it may seem, we are all benefiting from our outdated, limiting beliefs. There is a reason we have held onto them, negative as that reason might be. This can be difficult to admit, but it's true for me and it's true for you. In our own way we have held onto the past because it provides safety, comfort, security and minimum risk.

Old beliefs are keeping us in our place. They tell us not to rock the boat and that things are just fine the way they are. Fooled again.

These old beliefs play themselves out in work as they do in life. Work/business based on the Industrial Revolution model is meant to control and to encourage conformity. This outdated definition limits and devalues our potential, humanness and spirit, stifling what businesses now need most.

Everything starts with a belief, and our beliefs can change. At some point the pain of staying the same becomes greater than the pain of change. It is human nature to change and grow. We are not stagnant beings. Examining the past is the first step.

What the Past Has to Do with It (see next page)

Outdated & Limiting Beliefs	Current Outcome Based on this Belief	Benefit Gained - Why Belief Is Still Active	Source of Belief. It's NOT Yours!
1.			
2.			
3.			
4.			
5.			
6.			
7.			

B. Evolving Beyond Old Patterns –
Here's the <u>Challenge</u>:

Again, this Challenge is your time to step back and reflect. The exercises that follow are a prerequisite to the next section, so take the time needed. Duplicate the chart on the previous page for your answers.

Thanks,
Patricia

1. Think back to the past and the environment you grew up in. What was the belief system within your home and in society at the time? What were the statements and messages you heard about yourself, life and work/business that are still part of your world today? Write these down in column one. This may take time to surface, so don't rush.

2. In the second column, write down the current outcome of each belief. What is occurring in your life and work given this belief? What is the result? Again, if answers don't surface right away, you can come back later.

3. It is important to be clear on the reason these beliefs are still in your life. You are benefiting from them. This may be difficult to see, for often we don't want to admit this to ourselves, especially if that gain is reinforcing a negative pattern. In the third column, be easy on yourself and be honest as you write down whatever comes up.

4. In the last column, write down where those beliefs originated. Was it a parent, your religion, a friend or relative, society, etc.? Realize that the belief was not and is not yours. Stop owning it. Loosen its grip.

C. Maturing Takes Forgiveness

Many of the outdated beliefs you identified were developed as a result of various life experiences. In many cases, this is what we then base our lives on. The beauty is that now we can choose to release these beliefs to make room for the new and the wonderful.

Evolving into the future first takes shaking hands with the past. We need to come to terms with our past—not push it away. We want to loosen its grip and then release its hold. This will give us the wherewithal to shift our perspective into a new present. Only then can our life and work create our dreams and desires.

This part of the work isn't always so pleasant. It can be difficult to come face-to-face with the truth of the past. We would rather skip over it completely; but believe me, this work must be done.

There is an old adage that goes, "We live in either guilt from the past or fear of the future." We let the negative of the past hang on our shoulders like an unbearable weight. It taints every decision we make as we operate out of obligation, shame and a feeling of being not enough.

Of course all of this is a part of learning from life. These life lessons and experiences are a vital part of the carving out of our purpose. We are all given experiences—some utterly delightful, others painful and many life changing.

The painful experiences are the ones we want to now acknowledge, embrace and release. If we don't, they will surely work against us. When we refuse to see and then release painful experiences in our life, the blocked energy turns against us. Its power must go somewhere—if not purposefully outward, then destructively inward. We end up shutting down, getting depressed, and isolating ourselves in a small, lonely world.

For starters, take a minute to stand up and literally shake loose from the hands of the past. Just shake your body: your shoulders, back, arms, legs and head. Let those old burdens fall away. Take a few deep breaths and release them. Great!

Reconcile with the past. It will always be a part of who we are. In fact, there are many wonderful aspects of the past that desire honoring. But the aspects that drag us down may have served once, but now they're truly getting in the way.

Do know that there is much at stake in doing this. Our greater life and purpose are on the line. Our freedom and ability to leave the world a better place are up for grabs. Any part of us denied denies the whole, and the whole is the place from which our purpose blossoms.

Every last one of these life experiences has contributed toward evolution, toward surfacing the authentic self and ultimately toward shaping work/business purpose. This may be hard to admit because the pain and anger are deeply rooted. This may cause us to clutch even tighter making it harder to forgive and release.

> *The last 20 years of my life I've been on a journey that has taken me to both the heights and the depths of my existence. I've "remembered" experiences I've kept hidden up to now. These have been extremely painful—almost too hard to see. In facing this deeper level of truth, I've been able to see the isolation, abuse and shame that have kept me locked in old patterns.*
>
> *I have both thanked and cursed God for helping me see what I've been unwilling to face. These realizations created many tear-filled nights, have brought up a lot of anger and have often left me confused. I could no longer hide in denial, as we humans are so good at doing.*
>
> *When I was willing to come to terms with these experiences, their energy weakened, and the truth began to set me free. What had been holding me back, sabotaging my life and purpose, is now propelling me forward. The recognition of a deeper level of truth has given this blocked energy room to breathe. This is true freedom. I'm with you on this one, so don't give up.*

Only after we loosen the grip on the past can we then forgive. This is the next key step: forgive the past, the people and the circumstances that we see as having harmed us. Forgiving does not mean giving up or giving in—it means letting go. Forgiving comes from a deep sense and belief in humanity. It takes a big person to forgive, to let go of the hurt and anger and to embrace the humanness and imperfection in us all.

Without forgiveness we remain bitter and separated. We wind up hurting ourselves the most.

Desmond Tutu talks about the very essence of forgiveness in his book *No Future Without Forgiveness*. Forgiveness of the atrocities of apartheid. He argues that true reconciliation cannot be achieved by denying the past. He shows that through forgiveness we can move forward with honesty and compassion to build a newer and more humane world.

Forgiveness is a blessing that only we can give, and it starts with forgiving ourselves. As this happens we gain access to an emotional part of ourselves previously untapped. We open up to a new depth of aliveness that can now contribute to and become a part of our purpose.

As with everything in life, this process is ongoing. We don't just forgive once, we forgive again and again. We do the work, and then it circles back for us to take to the next level. It never ends but does get easier once we have gained the new awareness and tools needed.

Many of you are already doing this work. You have felt it, faced it and lived through it for the better. It is extremely hard to do in a vacuum so having a personal support system of like-minded individuals is helpful. Consider us part of this system. We honor the work you are doing. Your courage is appreciated.

Please complete the following exercises, for there is much at stake—your true work is on the line. Give this your full attention.

C. Maturing Takes Forgiveness – Here's the Challenge:

As I mentioned earlier, the Challenges are vital. Work through this one with an understanding friend, if that gives you comfort. There are seven steps to do, so take the time needed. Be patient as you call your life experiences to the surface. Don't wait. Act now. Your old self will want to talk you out of this, I guarantee. Don't listen. Just act!

Thank you so much,
Patricia

1. Identify and write down as many life-changing experiences as you can that have caused you pain, brought up internal conflict or confusion, or made you angry or sad. Search your mind, body and soul, and write down all that you can. These are the past experiences you want to unblock and release.

2. What might be stopping you from releasing the past and its blocked energy is anger, which is sometimes so deep you don't even know it's there. Do the following and see what surfaces. Go slow and be easy on yourself. Do this as often as necessary—today, tomorrow, next week or next month. You will quickly feel a loosening and letting go.

   Get angry! Take a pillow and pound your bed, scream in the shower, tear up old phone books (this is my favorite). As you do this, think about the experience and person you are angry at. Say out loud what you are angry about. Keep pounding, screaming or tearing, and release the anger from your mind and body. When you are done, close your eyes and let it all go. Breathe and release again and again.

3. Your anger has something to tell you. There is probably a lesson or two to learn. Grab your journal and ask your anger to express itself. Ask it what it wants to tell you. You will no doubt be surprised.

4. Close your eyes and, one by one, visualize releasing these negative experiences. Visualize putting what you wrote in #1 in a big helium balloon and then letting it go. Cut the ribbon that's attached to the balloon and let it float away. Breathe deeply and blow out. Blow the balloon away. You no longer need this experience to shape or influence your reality. Continue to breathe, blow and release the hold that each of these experiences has on you.

5. Now connect with how you feel after releasing this unwanted hold on you and your future. Do you sense a loosening, a letting go and even a new sense of freedom? Take a few moments and write about these feelings as you keep breathing and releasing.

6. Now comes the forgiving. You are going to work through this exercise twice. First, state who you want to forgive from your past and why you now need to forgive them. In the second pass, put your name after "I forgive: and state why you need to now forgive yourself. Think of the hurt you may have caused others first, then yourself, the judgment placed and the separation caused—innocently in most cases, but there.

Forgiving Others:

I forgive _____ for _____

I forgive _____ for _____

I forgive _____ for _____

I forgive _____ for _____

Forgiving Yourself:

I forgive _____ for _____

I forgive _____ for _____

I forgive _____ for _____

I forgive _____ for _____

7. Now take some time to appreciate yourself for a job well done. Take a warm bath or a hot shower, go for a long walk and be with nature, curl up to a good book with a cup of tea, or watch a funny movie. Do whatever you need to take good care of yourself.

D. PREDICTING YOUR FUTURE

We are now on our way. As we forgive the past and enlist it as an ally, we are freed to use these lessons to craft greater work/business in the future.

Work well done. Keep it up. It's now time to really stretch the boundaries of our work future. It *can* be what we desire, dream about and long for. Our passions and longings can become reality—one step at a time. Our highest potential can be realized in this world in the here and now.

We have been given the opportunity to literally create new work, work unlike this planet has seen to date. Work/business that is a path to our own evolution. Work not as a job, in a traditional sense, but as a means to learning life's lessons. Work/business as a natural extension of life that creates unity instead of separation and that is about purpose.

Be aware that a part of the dilemma is that we have been made to believe this can't be true. We've been told it's just the reverse, that what we see in the outer world—the jobs, careers and income desired—is what we have to work with. *It* is the point of all decision. We look to what currently exists and then try to determine how to best fit in—often a square peg in a round hole. This viewpoint is extremely limiting, when in actuality we can create from nothing. Who we uniquely are and what we desire *are* the source and foundation of life and work—not the limited external world.

Our future *is* of our making. It is built from choice—from the outcomes we desire framed in a set of NEW beliefs, new feeling and then NEW behaviors and actions. This is the foundation for the new work world: beliefs, feelings and behaviors that mold work/business that allows for a higher level of potential and a deeper level of humanity to shine. All three of these need to be clearly defined, claimed as ours to live into and affirmed as the desired future. Now, and only now, the magic can begin.

There is a saying that goes, "Be what you want most in life." As we "become" our desired future, it attracts itself to us.

Let's not waste time—the critical turning point is NOW. The following is a guide to a five-part process that, when done thoughtfully, will reap great rewards. As always, our longing needs to be strong, for this work is not for the faint of heart.

I would suggest reading through the following practices before going to the Challenge pages to note down your responses. This will give you a better sense of what is being asked of you before you delve deep into writing your responses.

> *"The notion of vocation comes from spiritual and philosophical traditions. It describes a "call," work that is given to us, that we are meant to do. We don't decide what our vocation is, we receive it. It always originates from outside us. Therefore, we can't talk about vocation or a calling without acknowledging that there is something going on beyond our narrow sense of self. It helps remind us that there's more than just me, that we're part of a larger and purpose-filled place."*
> — *"Turning to One Another: Simple Conversations to Restore Hope to the Future," Margaret J. Wheatley*

<u>First</u>: In the first section of this Tool you were asked to imagine yourself and your work or business as much more than it is now. You started with closing your eyes, putting a smile on your face and imagining a more self-assured YOU. What did you see when you did this? Recall that image in your mind's eye. See it as clearly as possible and know that it can happen now.

You can influence your future of choice by first gaining clarity on what you desire that future to look like. The following questions will stimulate your thinking.

✦ *What do you know without a doubt is needed in the marketplace that you could fulfill?*

✦ *What would you like to see and have happen in the work world that is not happening now?*

+ *What are you often pulled or called to do?*
+ *What do you do naturally?*

The first practice is visualizing all that you can see NOW, in the present moment—not tomorrow or two months from now, but this very moment. See it so you can BE it.

<u>Second</u>: This next practice is vital. After you see what you want, you need to BE it.

For example, if you visualize having partners in your life, then you need to first be a partner; if you want well-being and balance,

EVOLUTIONARY WORK CASE STUDY 2

MARY'S STORY

My roles changed very quickly. My degree classes were over. My son moved out into independence. I lost my father-in-law and my mom in the same year after intense interaction with their illnesses. My mother-in-law recovered in an assisted living residence and decided to stay on there. Empty home; no caregiving needed. I sensed an unnerving opportunity to question what was to be next. I took off a year to grieve and digest the changes. The silence was deafening, but I knew I had to sit on my hands and listen for direction. During the deaths and drained energy, I sought out the guidance of Patricia after reading about realizing one's life purpose. There were so many challenges and adventures I had experienced that I needed help in creating a new story, one that allowed me to feel and trust and get back to my spiritual roots. I needed to understand that although I felt uncomfortable I needed to focus on my needs and myself before I could reach out to others.

The prayer, meditation and silence, plus the homework, led me to visit a convent three miles from my home. (I had been part of a convent in my youth and left after nine years before taking final vows.) I asked to be taken to see the Sisters in the Infirmary. I felt an immediate peace. I began spending one day a week and developed an immediate,

then you need to bring well-being and balance into your life and the lives of others.

Therefore, based on your vision, you might start BEING...

✦ *A partner working side by side on projects with like-minded individuals where you all make a difference. You develop work that is a collective effort, serving everyone's greater potential.*

✦ *Flexible in how you create your workday and workplace so balance and well-being come first. Your day is one in which there is room for the artistic, musical, fun-loving aspects of who you are. You develop a workplace that honors your mind, body, emotions and spirit.*

✦ *A manifestation of your unique skills and talents, utilizing them so*

comfortable bond with these remarkable 80-95-year-old women. I brought "life" into their world with food and color and celebration. I soon realized in helping them find their spirit and expression that the fire began blazing within me. Being part of their convent family at 55 has been magical for both the Sisters and me. I have been there over three years now for two full days a week and have developed a much needed program based on self-expression and using voice, both repressed in this environment. Using my background and interest in nonverbal communication—and the use of dress and adornment to express who we are, how we feel and how we wish to be perceived—the Sisters, who are all still dressed alike, are a perfect study! Slowly we uncovered their individuality and true spirit, with a chance of voicing their purpose and possible legacies. We took the label off "infirmary" and "volunteer." (I prefer life-sharer.) My energy and spirit are like oxygen to them, and their wisdom, strength and humor are what inspire me.

With my background in education, a communication degree, business expertise and experience working with the senior population, both independent and infirmed, I am developing products and clothing that offer creative solutions that are functional but communicate individuality, spirit and expression. It is my theory that this creates more visibility, which will encourage interaction and feedback and have a direct correlation to an improvement in both physical and mental health and attitude. The Sisters' reaction? Their "expressed" feeling, like their collaboration, has made them feel like new pioneers!

they result in a business model whose services are highly desired and needed in the global marketplace and generate a substantial financial return.

✦ *Highly conscious of your thoughts, words and actions; well-aware and able to counteract your sabotaging patterns; and able to act on your wants and needs but not attached to the outcome.*

<u>Third</u>: Since everything starts with a thought, it's time to gain clarity on the new belief system needed to create the vision you desire. This demands getting clear on the thinking behind the being. What do you need to believe and think to have all that you envision for yourself and others?

You already worked on recognizing and releasing the old beliefs that keep you stuck in the past. Now get clear on your new beliefs.

As I write this I realize it would do me good to review my own beliefs, which change as I change. They are more positive and proactive than they have ever been. I'm quite sure there are lingering, sabotaging ones that still get in my way. It's time to recognize, heal and move out the outdated beliefs and up the ante on others. It's time to play the larger game!

I share the following with you to claim these new beliefs as ones I'm committed to:

1.   I "know" the power of this work and create a foundation and business model that feeds the pocketbook and soul for myself and many others that join with me to carry it out.

2.   I am a partner in all my life and work initiatives. I partner with many others to evolve ourselves and our work. I solidify the training of others to carry out this work.

3.   I am a wonderful public speaker, speaking worldwide and charging a valued fee.

4.   I bring my purpose to powerful, enlightened individuals, entrepreneurs and small businesses who are ready and willing to act on their next step to creating more purposeful work through Purposeful Business Circles worldwide.

5. I maintain a financial house that is in order, and my "wealth" is blossoming in leaps and bounds.

6. I honor my inner child through fun, movement, dance, being in nature and art.

7. I am more consciously conscious of my self-sabotaging patterns and choose to shift to new, healthy choices and actions. I know and honor my wants and needs.

Fourth: This next practice is as important as the "being" practice. This is the "feeling" practice. It's time to conjure up the feelings that accompany the success of your new, expanded beliefs. This may need some practice. The following techniques should help:

+ *Recall any time in the past when you felt successful.*
+ *Duplicate that feeling of success onto each of the new ways you are now being and onto your new beliefs.*
+ *Do this for each, one at a time. As you recall and regenerate the feeling, live in it and with it as long as possible.*
+ *Move the feeling into your everyday activities—hold onto it and keep it with you.*
+ *The last step is to act as if some magnificent, loving intelligence was waiting for you to accept all of these new ways of being, through a consciousness of faith, to then reveal your greater yet-to-be successful life and work!*

Fifth: Now comes the proof of the pudding, so please don't stop. What now needs to follow are the new behaviors and actions that demonstrate the inner change to the external world. If you know and understand the urgency of your purpose, your evolution and its ultimate impact in the world, then you will sense the urgency of this practice.

What actions are needed to mold the outcomes you desire? What are you willing to commit to—heart and soul—right now? Make your actions into commitments that are as concrete as possible, complete with milestones and deadlines.

The living picture of our work/business future, when planted in the present, can manifest into life and work beyond what we can imagine. Our new behaviors will cause our beliefs and feelings to occur in real time, transforming the essence of who we are. By affirming what the future can be on a daily basis, we will slowly breathe life into it. By acting on it, we will guarantee its place in the world.

"The future belongs to those who believe
in the beauty of their dreams."
– Eleanor Roosevelt

D. PREDICTING YOUR FUTURE – HERE'S THE <u>CHALLENGE</u>:

Now you are ready to start designing your future of choice. Now is the time to do the practices just mentioned. You may want to space this out and do these one at a time. The following require thinking from the future and acting in the present. Use the chart on the next page. As always, this Challenge is very important.

All the best,
Patricia

1. Visualize all that you are and all that you can be and do in the present moment. See it, then you can be it. What do you SEE?

2. Whatever you desire in your life will be attracted to you, but you must be it first. Who do you need to BE?

3. Determine the new beliefs needed to create the vision. What do you need to BELIEVE and THINK? These are "I" statements written in the present tense.

4. Step back and feel what would accompany the success of your new, expanded beliefs. To anchor these feelings, write about them with as much passion, description and emotion as you can. Go all out! What do you FEEL?

5. Here is where the proof of your work shows up. Please don't stop. Focus on the new behaviors and actions that will demonstrate the changes your want to occur. What BEHAVIORS and ACTIONS are needed?

Predicting Your Future

WHAT DO YOU SEE?	WHO DO YOU NEED TO BE?	WHAT DO YOU NEED TO BELIEVE & THINK?	WHAT DO YOU FEEL?	WHAT BEHAVIORS & ACTIONS ARE NEEDED?
1.				
2.				
3.				
4.				
5.				
6.				
7.				

TOOL 2

No Competition

A. *They Really Did Break the Mold*

B. *Tools for Uncovering Your Unique Work/Business Composite*

C. *Mind-Mapping New Work/Business Opportunities*

A. They Really Did Break the Mold

We have often heard that we are unique, but do you really believe it? Do you truly believe that you alone can live out the essence and energy of your unique purpose? You should, because it's true!

At some level we understand this, but the magnitude of this concept can be difficult to comprehend. The breadth, depth and power of our uniqueness are extremely compelling and can influence the lives of many.

Step back to take this all in, because it is often beyond the way we generally think about ourselves. If we truly lived from our uniqueness, wouldn't we act differently—more intentional, more focused and more at peace with ourselves?

How do we begin to wrap our head, heart and hands around this larger, deeper sense of self?

As a starting point, sit back, take a deep breath and digest the following statements. Don't just read them, say them aloud and breathe into them.

+ *I am unique.*
+ *There is no one else like me, nor will there ever be.*
+ *My life and work cannot be duplicated anywhere at any time.*
+ *If I don't live my purpose, no one else will.*
+ *My contribution to humanity can be demonstrated through my work.*
+ *I have this lifetime to make an impact.*
+ *THIS IS IT!*

What did it feel like to read this list? Good? Wonderful? Hard to believe? Was there any sadness because this may not be true for you right now? Do you have questions about the meaning and impact of this in your day-to-day life?

We often don't want to believe these truths. We tune out. Why? There are two reasons, which I'll explain in a minute. First, let's step back to observe our thinking. When we start to think about our purpose, our mind sometimes wanders. We tend to avoid, avert, deflect and close down in order NOT to think about this.

The mind says:

+ *What does this really mean to me in my life and work today?*
+ *Would I be fooling myself if I truly believed this?*
+ *Wow, what a responsibility.*
+ *I have no idea where to start.*

And so forth...

Why Do We Tune Out?

1) We have no mental frame of reference about ourselves and work in general that matches this expansive concept. We haven't been there before. Only after we develop the new mental wiring and belief systems that will accommodate this new frame of reference will we be able to see clearly. The truth of our uniqueness will then be quite apparent, and acting from this realization will come more naturally.

2) The unknown often makes us retract. We shrink into our "small" selves, into our need for security, safety and maintaining the status quo. We go back to living on automatic and rationalizing why.

I read once that we are the only species that can sabotage ourselves. We do it all the time by living in denial, seeing what we want then rationalizing our actions. We are experts at talking ourselves out of change.

> *As I sit, reflect and put pen to paper, I realize the immensity of this understanding and the huge undertaking ahead of us as a human race. There is much work to be done—on ourselves.*

Am I living my life as the one-of-a-kind human being that I am? What within me needs to shift to fully grasp this? How will this change my life?

There are many questions ahead of us. We will answer them one at a time. Be assured that the answers will come. Both the questions and the answers will assist us in developing the internal capacity to be our unique selves. This expanded frame of reference is built only from the ground up.

As we proceed, fear may surface about doing so. We are often afraid of our potential, power and purpose. We are afraid to see the truth because then we must act on it.

Can we live up to ourselves? Do we even try?

Our old identity is at stake—limited and outdated as it might be. We often feel that we can't jeopardize how others perceive us, how we perceive ourselves. If we start to question our sense of self, then who are we? To be without identity is frightening. We need to maintain our image so we can fit in, so we don't feel alone. Our fears can be so pervasive that we will do anything to stay the same.

However, evolution must run its course. This we can't stop. As we cling to what we know, everything around us is changing. Evolution is encouraging us to be all of who we are, our authentic selves.

We have no choice but to evolve. It is human nature, and we are powerless to resist, no matter what else we may think. It takes the form of "de-pressing" ourselves, bit by bit and day after day. Eventually the pain of staying the same will become greater than the pain of changing. Then and only then will we act.

"When you are inspired by some great purpose,
some extraordinary project,
all your thoughts break their bonds;
Your mind transcends limitations, your consciousness
expands in every direction, and you find
yourself in a new, great and wonderful world.
Dormant forces, faculties and talents become
alive and you discover yourself to be a greater
person than you ever dreamed yourself to be."
– Patanjali 1ˢᵗ to 3ʳᵈ Century

EVOLUTIONARY WORK CASE STUDY

MAJA

Retreats with Patricia

My first contact with Patricia was more than ten years back in Frankfurt, Germany. In the retreats she facilitated, she asked many powerful questions. This allowed me to think about myself in a new and helpful way. Her questions involved my mind and my heart. This gave me new insights into my life. She helped me identify my beliefs and made me aware that it was possible to decide which were helpful and which I better change.

Patricia also initiated a group work on our personal goals. In this group we meet every year for one day. We discuss what happened in the past year and what we want to go for this year. After many times with Patricia, we still meet in this development group since more than ten years.

A. They Really Did Break the Mold – Here's the <u>Challenge</u>:

The following questions are not easy. Your mind may resist, so be on the lookout. You may find that answering all of these questions in one sitting is too much. Try working in 20-minute blocks. You don't have to finish this section before you move on, but do finish it before the end of this Tool.

Thanks—you're doing great,
Patricia

1. If I truly believed I was one of a kind, what would this mean to my life and work/business?

2. What would I need and want to change? How might I BE different and what would I DO different if I was truly living from my innate gifts and talents?

3. What will get in the way of my making these changes? (Write down the potential internal and external roadblocks.)

B. Tools for Uncovering Your Unique Work/Business Composite

Once we realize we are one of a kind and understand the greatness, responsibility and power behind this, we are (hopefully) ready and motivated to take the next step: to bring life to our uniqueness and give it a purposeful form in the world that is viable and sustainable.

We are all a composite of talents and gifts, dreams and desires, education and experience, the whole of which makes up our uniqueness. When we take this composite view of ourselves, powerful new life and work possibilities emerge.

This process is often like putting together a puzzle for which you don't have all the pieces, so the picture is unclear and the result is an unknown. Don't let this scare you. Unknown doesn't mean never knowing. Trust this and let's move on.

Up to now, many of us have lived out our life and our work from a fragmented, compartmentalized framework. We have seen our life and work as separate activities utilizing separate skills. We still, overall, live in the 9-to-5, Industrial Revolution mental model of work/business. Our thinking, belief system and values are steeped in this outdated perception. However, as evolution would have it, we can no longer live in a framework that compromises the truth of our very existence—that is, our purpose and its place in the world.

This section of the book is going to introduce a number of new tools that will help you refine your sense of self to uncover the internal composite of attributes that make you unique. Each tool and process adds valuable insight to your new mental frame of reference and perception of self and greater work/business purpose.

B-1. CAPITALIZING ON CLUES & PATTERNS

From our very conception, life has been giving us clues to our uniqueness. They are evident in our emotions—what makes us smile as we dream about what's possible or what makes us sad as we long for our passion. We often miss these clues because we're not prone to believe in our dreams or ourselves and are distracted by the busy-ness of life.

As we become available to our purpose, a keener sense of life will start to unfold. We will see with new eyes and hear with new ears. In fact, all of our senses will reveal things about our uniqueness. Start by taking special note of:

+ *Recurring life and work occurrences.*
+ *Ah-has—insights that appear from out of the blue.*
+ *Things that make you happy or make you sad.*
+ *What connects you more to your true nature and just feels good.*
+ *What you love and have loved over the years.*
+ *Something that just won't leave you—like a thought, feeling or longing.*
+ *What comes to you in an easy, effortless, exciting way.*
+ *What you naturally give to others.*
+ *What ultimately makes your heart sing!*

Now, take a minute, close your eyes, take a deep breath and get a sense of what is coming up for you.

This is a good reminder for me because I, too, sometimes forget to pay attention to life and put up my internal antennas. The clues just fly by. I'm on automatic pilot, missing opportunities as I let my agenda take precedence. Moreover, there goes the day, week or month.

Be aware that these clues show you the full spectrum of life: the good and the not so good. Some may startle you, some you already know but may have forgotten, and some will be difficult to look at but ultimately helpful. These are the missing pieces to the puzzle. You will find that the clues could be anything. Don't censor what comes up if you can't see a direct and immediate correlation to your work/business. Remember, we tend to want to fit everything into the work framework we recognize and are most comfortable with. We can easily discard what is right in front of us because it doesn't fit our usual picture. Stay open to surprises.

B-1. Capitalizing on Clues & Patterns – Here's the <u>Challenge</u>:

Give yourself quiet reflection time to work on the following. As with all the Challenges, try working in 20-minute blocks. This section is about surfacing the bits and pieces of the puzzle—the attributes that make up your unique composite of skills and talents. This is the first of what I call ongoing Challenges because we want to make these new skills new habits. With practice, these habits will become second nature and a new expansive part of your everyday life.

Thanks,
Patricia

1. Put up your antennas, take a deep breath and reflect on the following statements relative to your unique composite. In response to each statement below, write down whatever comes to mind. Then go back over the list and, with a colored pencil or marker, circle what comes up repeatedly, what stands out and what now seems so obvious. Last but not least, use the puzzle format on the next page and fill in the pieces with your recurring insights. Feel free to put more than one insight per puzzle piece. (Don't be concerned if it still isn't clear. Just continue to the next section and have fun!)

+ *Recurring life and work patterns.*
+ *Ah-has—insights that appear from out of the blue.*
+ *Things that make you happy or sad.*
+ *What connects you more to yourself, what feels good to you.*
+ *What you love and have loved over the years.*
+ *Something that just won't leave you—like a thought, feeling, or longing.*
+ *What comes to you in an easy, effortless, exciting way.*
+ *What you naturally give to others.*
+ *What makes your heart sing!*

Unique Skills, Talents & Gifts

B-2. Asking the Next Right Question

The next "right" question is what leads us to deeper, more intensive inquiry into our purpose. The goal here is to reach the core to uncover our true attributes. Answers found at this level will both give us a greater picture of ourselves and provide us with a larger playing field for our work/business. This deep questioning process taps the wisdom of our purpose, allows us to see new work opportunities, ultimately expanding our choices in the marketplace.

When things get tough, though, we typically dig only so deep. We search for the quick fix, a resolution that may appease us for the moment but in the end does little to guide us toward deeper meaning. In order to evolve, we need to resist this business-as-usual tendency. What is called for is being more truthful and honest with ourselves.

Asking the next right question is not something we may have ever learned. We've learned to ask the same question with a little twist, to ask the next obvious question, or not to ask questions at all. We work from "What I don't know can't harm me" and therefore stay mute.

A deeper level of questioning is what will uncover new work. These are questions that:

+ *Challenge and expand our perception of ourselves and our work/ business.*
+ *Originate from a radically different point of view—beyond our norm.*
+ *Surface something that may at first seem odd, unusual or surprising.*
+ *Deepen and broaden our understanding of ourselves.*
+ *Are downright hard and sometimes painful.*
+ *Appear risky and almost impossible to answer.*
+ *Excite, startle and even make us laugh.*

*"Questions are more transformative than answers and are
the essential tools of engagement. They are the means by
which we are confronted with our freedom."*
– *"Community: The Structure of Belonging,"*
Peter Block

So where do we start? With our degree of willingness. Give yourself permission to run a test and dig deeper. Start with the first step. Here are a few questioning methods to help you get started:

1. <u>Dig three levels deep</u>—State the initial question, determine the response, then ask yourself "why" of the reply. Your answer will be "because…Now again ask "why." Now repeat this "why" one more time. By the time you come up with the third "why" response, you will have tapped a deeper core and surfaced a more meaningful insight.

    What makes me really good at this particular skill? And why am I good at that? Now, why am I good at that?

2. <u>Project into the future and act today</u>—First envision yourself 3–5 years from now. What do you see? Now, ask yourself if who you are and what you are doing today is heading you in this direction. If not, why not?

    Will my current beliefs and actions get me to my vision of the future? If not, what am I willing to change now?
    If I start being and doing something different, such as ____ and ____, then how will that impact my life and work/business in 3–5 years?

3. <u>Question your heart and head</u>—I've heard that the best decision is made when your head and heart agree. So, when you are faced with a decision, first ask your heart and note the response then ask your head again noting your response. What is middle ground?

What does my heart have to say about that? What does my head have to say? What is the middle ground?

4. Ask a question you are afraid to ask—I have found that doing one thing different every day that I'm afraid to do definitely builds my risk-taking muscle.

   What do I fear the most that I need to act on now? What might be the benefit of moving ahead when I'm afraid to do so?

5. Think forward—If you find yourself in "circular thinking," which is an endless loop of *what if* this and *what if* that, then grab those thoughts and ask a question that will move them forward.

   What best action will move me forward? What is the next "right" step I can take?

6. Ask a larger, more all-encompassing question—If you find yourself playing too small, then ask a question that is larger in scope—more global and all-encompassing.

   If I started describing myself from what makes me unique, how might I introduce myself? If I truly think globally then act locally, what is my next right step? Who do I need to be and what do I need to do to get my work/ business out to a larger audience?

7. Ask a question that truly evokes passion—Tapping and surfacing your passion will always move things forward.

   What truly makes my heart sing? What could I not live without "being" or "doing"? What stirs me to tears or to anger?

8. Ask yourself a more honest question—You do know what I mean! We often know the next right question but don't want to face it. I believe this is the most important questioning method of all.

Am I truly using my gifts and talents in my work? If not, why not? What higher risk do I know I need to be taking now?

The following are a series of questions on 'gifts' that Peter Block, as previously referenced, states in his book. They truly exemplify the asking the next right question process. Try them out for size.

+ *What is the gift you currently hold in exile?*
+ *What is it about you that no one knows about?*
+ *What are you grateful for that has gone unspoken?*
+ *What is the positive feedback you receive that still surprises you?*
+ *What is the gift you have that you do not fully acknowledge?*

The skill of asking the next right question and the methods given can serve you well, so take higher risk, conjure up the courage and start now.

> *Asking the bigger, more honest question will require more risk taking, more venturing into the unknown, and will force me to have more faith in myself and my work. I'll need to value my work at a higher level.*
>
> *A friend recently reminded me of the value of the work that we each do. She is a knitter and creates wonderful wearable art pieces. She was sharing a story with me about a woman she met in a similar trade who talked about her work in such a caring way—she cherished her work like we would a child. The value she gave to it was priceless, the beauty that shone through was marvelous, and the belief she had in it was not up for debate. So this is what I will practice and also ask you to practice: cherish yourself and your work; hold it as precious and priceless, and present it as such.*

The challenge here is to *always* be asking yourself the next right question. Make this practice a new habit so it starts to replace the old wiring. Your life and your work/business will then become a reflection of the next right question and the next right answer will automatically surface.

B-2. Asking the Next Right Question – Here's the Challenge:

Asking the next right question will help you surface a deeper level of your unique composite. Practice using these questioning methods over the next two to three weeks, and make them a habit. Do the following, and don't forget to use your journal.

Keep up the good work,
Patricia

First: Use the questioning methods below and keep track of your answers.

Second: Go back over your answers and circle the recurring patterns.

Third: Add these to your puzzle from the last section.

+ *Dig three levels deep*
+ *Project into the future and act today*
+ *Question from your head and heart*
+ *Ask a question you're afraid to ask*
+ *Think forward*
+ *Ask a larger, more all-encompassing question*
+ *Ask a question that truly evokes your passion*
+ *Ask yourself a more honest question*

C. Mind-Mapping New Work/ Business Opportunities

Opportunities for purposeful work and businesses abound. They are around every corner, behind every fence and within every person. It's up to us to recognize the ones that are ours to be and act on.

We are today and always have been blessed with unique attributes. We are a sum of all the lessons learned from the past, all that we are called to be and do in the present, and all the dreams and desires of the future. This sum total, or composite, births our purpose.

By now your puzzle is surely overflowing. As we continue to look more deeply, the unique expression of who you are in the world will surely surface. Work, with a capital W, that is the largest expression and evolution of YOU is what we are after.

You are a culmination of all the attributes that have surfaced during the deep inquiry of the last two sections. The clues and patterns that surround you can no longer be ignored, and the next "right" question beckons you to look beyond what's apparent to a deeper level of self.

When these attributes are creatively pulled together and combined in unique ways, what will surface are new and exciting work/business opportunities that will surprise and delight you. New actions are then up to you.

So put on your creative wisdom cap and let's continue.

C. Mind-Mapping New Work/ Business Opportunities – Here's the Challenge:

We want to jump right into this section and start the Challenge. It's time to pull together your puzzle "to date" to gain insights into what's possible.

What have you uncovered about YOU? What composite of characteristics makes you unique? What are the truth and the greatness about you?

Before starting this Challenge, create an enlivened environment— play music, pull out colored markers and make it fun. Give yourself plenty of time. It may take a couple of passes to complete.

This Challenge consists of four steps:

1. Creating a mind-map
2. Asking strategic questions about what you drew and wrote
3. Matching your mind-map against needs in the marketplace to create new work
4. Identifying your top choices

Thanks,
Patricia

Step One – Create the mind-map

(Please read through the following before getting started.)

1. Let's first learn a little about mind-mapping. (Do know that the following is my definition adapted for our use.) Mind-mapping is a circular, non-linear way of putting pen to paper. It is a form of outlining, note-taking and/or creative brainstorming done in a circular fashion. The process taps our more creative nature and

whole brain, making the output more global and innovative in nature. It's a free-form exploration with a focus. For our use, the focus is on your unique composite.

2. Use the next page to start your mind-map. Write the focus of your map in the circle at the center; e.g., Uniqueness, Your Name, Composite of Attributes, etc. Then start drawing lines, like spokes in a wheel, coming out from the circle. Leave space between each spoke for a second part that we'll go over in #4.

3. Now, on each line write an attribute from your puzzle. Each line represents one of your unique skills, talents and/or gifts. Write as many attributes as you like. If you are feeling really expansive, start with a larger piece of paper.

4. Now, focusing on one attribute at a time, ask yourself why that unique attribute is important—important to you, to others and/or to the world in general. Write your response under the spoke on a slanted line. Now going three levels deep, do this two additional times, asking why this attribute is important and writing down your response. In total you will have three responses under each attribute.

For example: If "public speaking" is one of your attributes, then write it on one of the spokes. Now ask yourself why speaking is important. Your responses might be something like "it's a way of expressing what I believe"; "through speaking I can share my knowledge and wisdom"; "speaking is a way to impact many people." Write all three responses on slanted lines under the spoke.

Creating your mind-map is meant to help you see the essential nature of each attribute as well as its importance to you and others. Upon completion, go to the second step.

Mind-Mapping New Work/
Business Opportunities

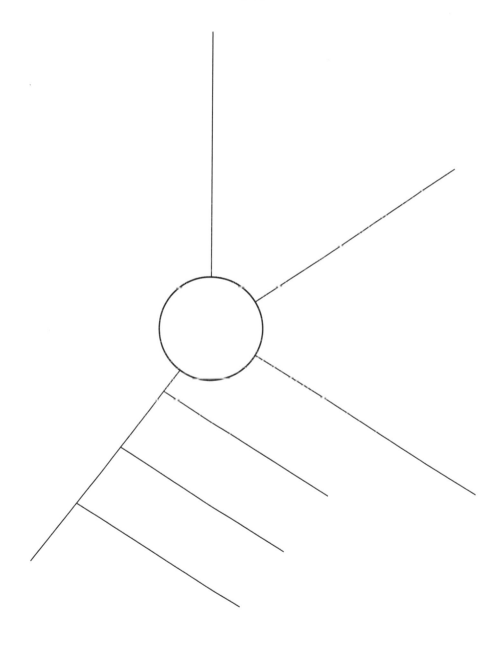

Step Two – Ask strategic questions about your mind-map

Now we're going to step back to further analyze your mind-map. By doing the following you will gain additional input about your purpose in the marketplace.

1. Rank each attribute starting with the number one. Write this number ranking on your mind-map. Rank them based on the amount of energy and passion you possess for each. You can also do this based on the importance of your responses to asking why-why-why.

2. Then ask the following: What commonalities and patterns do you see between or amongst the attributes? Write your responses. For instance, you may notice similarities of attributes that keep repeating themselves. What is this telling you? Is acting on these attributes essential to your well-being and happiness?

3. What additional new awarenesses popped up for you along the way? Write them down; anything goes.

Step Three – Match your mind-map against needs in the marketplace to create new work

Now we want to do big picture, creative thinking to come up with new work/business possibilities. By combining two, three or even four of your attributes in a creative way, a new work or business idea might surface. If you combine the attributes that you ranked as most vital you might come up with a work focus you hadn't previously realized.

For example, if you list attributes of public speaking, travel and animals, then maybe working as an international speaker on animal rights might be exciting. If your top three attributes are swimming, writing and technology, maybe you could create interactive web-based swimming instructions for a school system.

Now, at first your ideas may seem far-fetched, but don't stop now.

Use your journal to write down every idea that surfaces. DO NOT CENSOR. Just stay in the flow of new ideas; and, as always, anything goes.

Step Four – Identify your top choices

Upon completion, rank-order your list and hold the top three or four as most important as we move forward. Begin to see them as possible and even probable in the marketplace.

TOOL 3

CREATING A STRONG FOUNDATION

A. *No Doubt About It*

B. *Stop Fooling Ourselves – Work ≠ Security*

C. *New Tools = New Foundation = New Work*

D. *Beyond Self-Deception to Self-Realization*

A. No Doubt About It

*"To be nobody but yourself in a world that is doing its best
to make you just like everybody else means to fight the
greatest battle there is to fight and to never stop fighting."*

e.e. cummings

The last Tool was meant to give you a glimpse of what's possible as new work in the world. This Tool is meant to build a foundation to support that work. As it may have become clear, the Seven Evolutionary Tools are designed to evolve you into higher potential toward more purposeful work. This demands a courage that will withstand the winds of change, the well-intended naysayers and our own self-doubt. What is being called for is a new strength—a strength that comes from a deeper place—and a realization that our work or purpose is a force that can change the world.

We have been led to believe that strength was about controlling our outer world and using our will to create our work reality. The source of this strength came from brute force, power over others and fear. With this strength we used and manipulated work through our personality, positions and money. We operated as if this was the only way to succeed—and at some level, it certainly appeared that way.

We have evolved beyond this concept. It will not support the work of the future. Our new strength originates from our inner lives, rooted in greater self-knowledge, wisdom and humanity.

We are at a critical turning point in the world of work, and a decision is at hand. Are we going to continue to allow the old fear-based strength to take the lead? Do we conduct business as usual? Or do we dare to play a larger game, founded on inner strength and a mental model of self and work that serves all?

Developing a new inner strength is one of the many essential tools to creating new work. A rock-solid strength will keep us grounded. This is what I mean by "no doubt about it."

The deeper and stronger our foundation, the greater the work we will be given. The more work we do on ourselves, the more we can assist others. This spiral passes through a deeper level every time. The saying holds true that "We can't take others to where we haven't first gone ourselves."

Do we have what it takes? Can we counteract centuries of control and step out into the marketplace to develop work that focuses on people, profits and the planet? Together we can!

A. No Doubt About It –
Here's the Challenge:

Take on the following Challenge as a means to this new strength.

Thank you ahead of time for your willingness to do this work,
Patricia

1. In order to develop "new" inner strength you need to know what triggers the outdated. In the workplace, when do you find yourself in power over others—making yourself right and others wrong; manipulating the situation for your good in neglect of others; using your personality, position or money to control? Write about this.

2. Running a Test: For a day or longer, act as if you have a sense of "No Doubt About It" with respect to yourself and your work. Feel the feelings that accompany this new strength. You are confident, courageous and strong. At the end of the day write about what was different

B. STOP FOOLING OURSELVES – WORK ≠ SECURITY

The shift from the old outer to new inner strength creates a fundamental change in the very root of our security and serenity. We thought that as long as we had enough money in the bank, a job that paid well and a portfolio that increased yearly that our security was guaranteed.

This false dependency has jeopardized both our lives and our work. It has put our decisions in the hands of others. We play a game based in the fear of losing what we think is most important, we abdicate, play nice and play deaf. Bargaining with our talents, time, dreams and desires comes at a dear price.

Like it or not, our only true security stems from a rich inner life and connection to a power greater than ourselves. This inner life is developed through a responsibility to our purpose, our potential and our selves.

But work as security has a strong hold. When confronted with the question of security, our old tapes will chatter loudly:

+ *"She just doesn't understand that I have a family to take care of";*
+ *"I want to make some changes but don't want to sacrifice my lifestyle";*
+ *"I can't take the risk – you are just asking far too much";*
+ *"What will others say? They'll think I've gone soft."*

I've heard it all before—in myself and in others—that persistent voice inside that says: "Face the facts, Patricia, you aren't making enough money"; "You don't know what you are doing. Who do you think you are?" This rattling plays on my sense of security. Do I compromise myself to do work that pays the bills, or do I hold out and do what I know I must? For me there doesn't seem to be a choice. Holding out is always what I end up doing.

As we learn to shift our reference point, we become more grounded in ourselves. The old mental tapes begin to quiet down. Our resolve strengthens. Life and work become easier.

As Nathaniel Branden Ph.D., author of *The Art of Living Consciously* and *Six Pillars of Self-Esteem,* who is quoted extensively in this section, so astutely puts it, "One of the most important moments is when the client grasps that 'no one is coming.' No one is coming to save you; no one is coming to make life right for you; no one is coming to solve your problems. If you don't do something, nothing is going to get better."

B. STOP FOOLING OURSELVES – WORK ≠ SECURITY – HERE'S THE <u>CHALLENGE</u>:

The challenge is to first recognize that we often base our security on things other than ourselves. We do this all the time, in many large and small ways. One step at a time we will get there together.

Thanks,
Patricia

1. On what do you base your sense of security that may not be healthy or rightfully earned or is codependent? Check off as many of the following that apply, then write a few sentences as to why.

   I place my security in my…

   ___ Job/Work   ___ Career   ___ Superior

   ___ Board of Directors   ___ Coworkers   ___ Education

   ___ Title   ___ Economic Status   ___ Business

   ___ Organization   ___ Home Ownership ___ Bank Account

   ___ Other Areas: _____

   Why?

2. What would happen if you consistently shifted the reference point of security from outside yourself to inside? Write down the inner reference points you already access and use often. For example, your knowledge of your strengths and your gifts, your trust in a higher power and the ability to stay in the present.

C. New Tools = New Foundation = New Work

We are the new footing and structure for new work. Part of this core is our consciousness and sense of inner security. Next is our inner foundation, and as with any foundation, the broader and deeper it is, the more it can bear and the more comfort it brings.

With the help of author Nathaniel Branden, I have assembled the following as a vehicle for building our foundation. I call these the *tools of the self.* When consciously developed, these tools will rebuild our work footing. Starting from the ground up, the shape and form of our foundation expands. The end result is a deeper sense of trust in ourselves and our purpose, as well as the courage to act.

The core tools are **self-awareness, self-acceptance, self-responsibility, self-discipline** and **self-assertiveness**—in that order. These tools result in yet another set—**self-esteem, self-respect, self-efficacy** and **self-love**. And we can't neglect the flip side—**self-doubt, self-denial** and **self-sabotage**. We need to and will address all of these. These all culminate into the ultimate tool of self-mastery.

In many cases these tools have been used to reinforce a sense of self developed from a false state of being. We have been *told* to be responsible and assertive by our parents, school, religious systems and, of course, our work environments. This "being told" from the outside-in leads to codependence.

The old *shoulds, oughts* and *musts* can do more harm than good. These new tools are now needed to create a different frame of reference. Their root is first in self then in relation to work and others. They arise from within as a result of a new work passion, desire and purpose. They provide us with the choice, and thus the freedom, to do what we must to create our work.

Taking an honest look at today's workplace shows us that these tools aren't widely used. If they were, the workplace would be different. It would be a place where:

1. Each individual directs his or her own destiny;
2. We each take responsibility for our livelihood, growth and development;
3. Self-actualization is commonplace;
4. We don't operate from denial or rationalize our decision making;
5. We act from the greater good;
6. People, profits and the planet is the triple bottom line.

When we give ourselves permission to operate at this deeper level and practice these tools on a daily basis, the work world will be different. It will be a place of human dignity and integrity, growth and kindness. "Business needs to be the incubator of the human spirit," as is so poignantly said in *New Paradigms in Business*, published by The World Business Academy. Business will become the incubator of human evolution, where our learning and growth is supported. This will, by its nature, build self-esteem, self-respect, self-love and self-efficacy.

Exploring the tools of the self would not be complete if we didn't look at the flip side, which some call the shadow side. If we neglect to look at all aspects of our selves and our businesses, we will be ignoring a side that follows us wherever we go, unrecognized and undefined.

Our ability for self-doubt keeps us small and in hiding. In the workplace we "hide" our potential and humanity, as we also hide our fear and anger. This destroys our self-esteem and crumbles our self-respect. Everyone loses. Our work becomes stagnant, and we lose touch with ourselves in the process. When this happens, we have truly sold our souls.

In the following sections we will focus on the "whole" self. As we do this, our work will blossom. We will no longer need the outer world as proof of our existence—our work will be an inside job.

C-1. Consciousness

Aprerequisite to cultivating the *tools of the self* is a deepened sense of consciousness. Without it we wouldn't be aware of the need for these tools or be able to act on them.

Some initial questions about consciousness that may arise:

✦ *How do we know when we are living consciously?*

✦ *What are the distinctions?*

✦ *How do we discern this since we are so good at fooling ourselves?*

✦ *What does this have to do with work or business?*

Let's explore these questions by first exploring what living consciously actually means. The following is a definition by Nathaniel Branden.

"Living consciously is a state of being mentally active rather than passive. It is the ability to look at the world through fresh eyes. It is intelligence taking joy in its own function. Living consciously is seeking to be aware of everything that bears on our interests, actions, values, purposes and goals. It is the desire to discover our mistakes and correct them. It is the quest to keep expanding our awareness and understanding, both of the world external to self and of the world within. It is respect for the distinction between the real and the unreal. It is the commitment to see what we see and know what we know."

It is not a reaction but an undertaking based in awareness. Again, Nathaniel Branden: "The essence of consciousness is respect for reality. It is based on will and choice. It is a feeling as it is also an experience— an interplay between self and life. Living consciously entails paying attention to the relationship between our professed values, goals and purposes and our daily behavior."

What comes to mind is the saying "walk our talk." Many businesses have their mission statement posted high so everyone can see, especially their customers. In reality, there is no semblance of their mission in the day-to-day workings. The question that surfaces is why do *we* unconsciously buy into this? Maybe it's because we would like it to be true. We would like to see businesses operate from a higher mission. Our wishing it was true is not going to make it happen. This is a prime example of the dire need to raise our level of consciousness.

EVOLUTIONARY WORK CASE STUDY
VERNESTINE LAUGHINGHOUSE
Purposeful Business Circle Member

The strength and self-confidence to continue my business was shaken apart with the recession. Before the recession, I'd always believe that I had the solution to any problem that I might face. It was a good time for self-reflection and building. I could not determine the best method to get business, which really caused me to go in many different directions for about nine months. During that time I wasn't really thinking strategically about the business; I was just going any direction that the wind blew. I wondered if this was still the business I was supposed to be in. I questioned if it was time to throw in the towel and go back to the world of being an employee. Each time that thought crossed my mind, that feeling deep down told me no, not yet. This is what you enjoy—not just this type of business, but the flexibility it offers.

I built my self-confidence and strength by going back to the basics of what I did when I started the business: networking, strategically looking for opportunities, contacting past clients and a lot of self-reflection.

I started attending the Purposeful Business Circle, which has helped me to look at not just the business but myself. I'm getting more from it than I expected. I attended my first Circle to simply get out and be around positive people.

Each Circle that I attend gives me something I need. I needed ideas to grow my business; I got them from the other members. I need encouragement to change my way of thinking and being; I got it. When I needed a push in an area that I didn't know about myself, I got it. The conversations have led me to self-reflection, which in turn assisted with personal growth.

I can always get what I need by being a part of the Purposeful Business Circle.

I know I'm living consciously whenever I feel a sense of inner peace regardless of what's happening around me with work or the world in general. When I've taken the time to ask the next "right" question or feel truly connected to others, I'm conscious. Whenever I know at a deep level that I am part and parcel of a larger world and that the world is a part of me, I'm conscious.

When I'm stressed, afraid or rushed, my automatic reaction takes over and I find myself making poor business decisions, stuck in my "better than" stance. I'm in my old thinking, operating from business as usual. This lack of consciousness prevents new choices from appearing on my radar screen.

The traditional model of work has limited respect for consciousness. It often views taking time to reflect as a luxury that business can't afford. It believes that we need to react and react fast to the pressure and demands of customers, bosses and stockholders. I'm not saying we don't need to respond to these demands, but if we do this from a conscious state we will unearth the much-needed new answers to our old problems, changing patterns that continually repeat the past.

There is no choice for me and possibly no choice for you. You may have also "hit the wall" for the hundredth time and are saying "no more." No more of this foolishness—how long can we live in a state of lies about what work is about? There is no choice but to change, for at stake are the lives of individuals whose work environment worsens daily. The old economic model of work is showing signs of its own demise. The number of corporate scandals and an economy that couldn't get much worse are all signs of the death of a way of work that no longer serves us. If this is not a wake-up call for change, then I'm not sure what is. Hopefully, since the pain has now hit our finances, stock market and retirement plans, we will be more willing to do something about it. We tend to change when we are in enough pain.

You will note, though, that we still resist. If we have no choice and there is so much at stake, then what are we kicking and screaming about? What is this resistance? We resist because to make way for the new we must let go of the old.

The price of freedom is letting go of the comfort of an unhealthy work situation in which complacency has taken over. We know, at some level, that it is hard work to stay conscious. Have we become lazy or too busy for our own health and growth?

We need to be "consciously conscious" as my dear friend Ishwar Bhavnani always reminds me. This is the foundation for the "tools of the self."

C-1. CONSCIOUSNESS –
HERE'S THE CHALLENGE:

How do we consistently be "consciously conscious" so we act from a deep sense of awareness? How do we make work decisions from concern and compassion and not just from the bottom line? How do we consciously get beyond fear as the motivator?

Please answer the following questions to raise awareness and raise consciousness.

Thanks,
Patricia

1. What does living and working consciously mean to you? Be as descriptive as possible.

2. How "consciously" conscious are you on a daily base? What within you inhibits this?

3. What can you do to make consciousness your major MO (mode of operation)?

C-2. Tools of the Self

The ways of the command-and-control work model are now being traded in for tools rooted in the individual and purpose. These tools are at our fingertips, but we need to reconfigure them so they'll do their magic at the depth necessary. They will be part of our new toolkit. With practice, practice and more practice, they will drive new habits toward new work.

There are five core tools that will become our new foundation: **self-awareness**, **self-acceptance**, **self-responsibility**, **self-discipline** and **self-assertiveness**. Don't be fooled into believing you have mastered these.

> *I thought I knew what these five core tools meant and therefore believed I either had them or was working on all of them. Was I wrong! I think of myself as self-aware, so I was quite surprised when I went searching for a definition of self-awareness and found more than I bargained for. I always thought self-awareness meant knowing your gifts, talents, dreams and desires.*

But according to Nathaniel Branden, "self-awareness deals with the concern to understand the inner world of needs, motives, thoughts, mental states, emotions and bodily feelings."

SELF-AWARENESS

"If we are to function effectively, we must learn
to look in two directions: to preserve contact
with the world and with the self."
– "The Art of Living Consciously,"
Nathaniel Branden

Being as infinite as the galaxies and as complex as DNA, we are never or rarely ultimately self-aware. There is always more to know. It is human nature to grow and learn. Our job is to dig deep and broad with a goal that's nothing short of wisdom. As we begin to "know what we don't know" about ourselves, we are more confident, courageous and truthful. In turn, our lives and our work become more focused and purposeful.

It takes time to reinvent our identity. The wanting and willingness must both be present. So here are some questions to think about:

1. To what extent do you know yourself?
2. What aspects of self serve you and at the same time others?
3. Where is the pain—where is the joy?
4. What could you not live without doing?
5. Where is your soul guiding you?

Those who can honestly answer all these questions are a rare breed—you have done your homework. If you answered a good number of them, you're making progress. If stumped, please continue.

As mentioned earlier, what follows is modeled after the work of Nathaniel Branden. His many books on cultivating the self have been an inspiration, as well as a source of daily practice, for me and my clients. Start to give thought to the following and we will do more later.

SELF-AWARENESS CHALLENGE:

The following are called sentence completion exercises. We start with sentence fragments, and you supply the endings. Write down whatever comes up. Don't judge yourself or censor your responses. Starting with self-awareness, let's try out the following sentences.

Thanks,
Patricia

1. At the beginning of each day for five days, come up with 6–10 endings for one of the following sentences. The endings can repeat themselves.

   ✦ *If I lived and worked from a greater level of self-awareness, I would...*
   ✦ *If I were more self-aware, I would know that my uniqueness rests in...*

2. Next—at the end of those five days, write 6–10 endings for the above using the following format:

   When I reflect on how I would feel if I *(place the sentence fragment here)*, then...

3. Now, at the end of the five days, go back and reread what you have written, then write down 6–10 endings for the following:

   If any of what I wrote is true, it would be helpful if I...

SELF-ACCEPTANCE

Self-acceptance is being okay with ourselves. The dilemma is knowing what "being yourself" means. There are many levels from which we can know and accept ourselves. Most individuals don't venture beyond the surface, sometimes afraid to find out what is underneath. Some fear that they won't find much, that there is nothing of value deep down inside, that they have no unique purpose. Won't they be surprised? Because the exact opposite is true.

There are usually certain caveats around self-acceptance. We tend to accept what we like and ignore all else. We accept the "acceptable" aspects of self relative to what is kosher in our work world. The rest we put under the covers and pretend don't exist. We put on our blinders and filter out all that we don't want to face.

This causes us to downplay both ends of the spectrum. We dismiss our imperfections as well as our talents. We do ourselves a great injustice. When we are willing to see and embrace one aspect of self, we can do the same for the other. We can have equal-opportunity insight! I call this "seeing the truth of reality." From acceptance comes growth, possibility and opportunity.

> "If we can see ourselves the way we are, that is
> the first step toward self-acceptance. Once we
> are able to accept ourselves just the way we are,
> everything can start changing from that point."
> – "The Mastery of Love," Don Miguel Ruiz

Individuals who "are" themselves and accept themselves stand out from the crowd. They are the innovative ones, the risk takers. They play a larger game without fear of reproach. Building our self-acceptance is essential to creating purposeful work and meaningful work environments—our task in the next Challenge section.

SELF-ACCEPTANCE CHALLENGE:

Honesty is key as you work through the following Challenge exercises. As always, there is no hurry.

Thanks,
Patricia

1. Answer the following. Write what immediately comes to mind—no censoring.

What aspects of yourself...
+ *Do you openly relish?*
+ *Are you indifferent about?*
+ *Could you do without?*

2. Answer the following questions:
+ *What would happen if you accepted all of what you just wrote down?*
+ *If you capitalized on all aspects of yourself in your work/business, what positive things might transpire?*

SELF-RESPONSIBILITY

We are the authors of our choices and actions. We have the ability to influence our existence and attain our goals. Self-responsibility is taking responsibility for the outcome of your life and work. If we up the notch a bit, we find it also means being responsible for our part in this time of evolutionary change. We are responsible for doing our part toward developing work that is purposeful, workplaces that are healthy and work relationships that are rich and meaningful.

This enlightened definition of self-responsibility is based on an inner knowing. It plays out when we:

✦ *Have a goal to live as consciously as possible*

✦ *Aim each day to make a difference in the lives of others*

✦ *Are constantly challenging ourselves to learn, grow and evolve*

✦ *Are working from a sense of honesty and integrity*

✦ *Aim to make our life and work reflect our purpose*

The traditional definition of responsibility tends to lock us into distorted beliefs. We think being responsible means we *should* listen to our boss, we *ought* to arrive at work earlier and we *must* stick to our deadlines. Not to say these things aren't important, but there is a more profound definition of responsibility that encourages us to live and work from a deeper place. This is where we choose to listen to our boss because he or she has our greater good in mind, we arrive at work early because we are excited about the difference we are making, and we stick to our deadlines because we know the benefit will impact many. This mind-set is very different than the first. We need to look at which we choose to live and work by.

This can be a very fine line, and it's easy to trick ourselves into believing we are responsible when we are working hard, paying the bills and taking care of our families. When business is the business of living our lives to the fullest, life and work take on a different focus. Self-responsibility is demanding more of us than ever before. This doesn't necessarily make life easier. Life becomes harder at first, because *we* are the only ones truly responsible for the outcome. If I dislike my work, then it's up to me to initiate a change. If the attitude of a colleague irritates me, I can either say something or change my reaction, and if I don't feel my work is very purposeful, then I have to go inside and find out why.

Some feel it's easier to play dumb and not care to know. Why are people not self-responsible?

- ✦ *They don't know that they aren't.*
- ✦ *They know they need to be but don't know how and/or choose not to learn how.*
- ✦ *They know they have the choice but don't want the responsibility.*
- ✦ *They know how, but it's easier to blame others, or they aren't motivated to make the necessary changes.*

Coming from a society that is highly codependent, many people have never had to learn to be self-responsible. The old model of life and work took care of it all. This outdated model is falling by the wayside, and an interdependent model is here to stay. We all need to get on this bandwagon.

When I asked a couple of clients how they are being self-responsible with their work and purpose, I received the following responses:

Mary, a client in Pittsburgh, PA—*After doing a lot of personal work, I now have the clarity to move forward on my purpose. I now know that my purpose, services and products are needed. Now is the time for change. I feel an urgency to be more purposeful. I feel a greater responsibility, because I recognize my gifts, and now I have a certain window of time to get them out. I also now have a greater respect for my innate talents and have seen how I can help others and want to help many more.*

Teri, a client in Los Angeles, CA—*I'm being responsible for my self-fulfilling purpose by:*
- ✦ *Planning and monitoring my activities weekly against my life purpose "wheel"*
- ✦ *Keeping a journal and writing down insights or key lessons as they occur*
- ✦ *Pushing myself beyond my comfort zone in order to grow*
- ✦ *Being "self-full," not selfish*
- ✦ *Being authentic in my interactions with others*

*"Taking responsibility for one's own part
in creating the present situation is the
critical act of courage and engagement, which
is the axis around which the future rotates."*
– *"Community: The Structure of the Belonging"*

SELF-RESPONSIBILITY CHALLENGE:

This tool can be a tricky one, so pay close attention as you proceed. Be true to yourself as you answer the following.

*Keep up the good work—I am here to support you,
Patricia*

Reflect on the following statements about self-responsibility, and complete them as honestly and thoroughly as possible.

1. Being true to myself through my work looks like…
2. When I maintain my ideals in my work, I'm able to…
3. Seeing my part in all encounters allows me to…
4. When I am living and working from a sense of purpose, I'm able to…
5. After reflecting on my answers to the above, the actions I will take are…

SELF-DISCIPLINE

"Self-discipline is the ability to organize our behavior over time in the service of specific tasks. Self-discipline requires the ability to defer immediate gratification in the service of

*a remote goal. This is the ability to project
consequences into the future—to think, plan
and live long-range. Neither an organization
nor a business can function effectively, let
alone flourish, in the absence of this practice."*
— "The Six Pillars of Self-Esteem"

Self-discipline is the ability to create a foundation and structure so life and work work *for* us, not *against* us. It's a tool used to help us achieve our work goals and stick to our agenda. Lacking this ability, we succumb to the ideas and objectives of others. Lack of discipline makes us vulnerable to these distractions.

Self-discipline is not the same as self-control. Self-control is when we restrain ourselves; self-discipline is about aligning ourselves to our pursuit and purpose and doing what is necessary to get there. It's the tool in our kit that helps us set priorities, meet deadlines, and be and feel accomplished.

This tool is vital to the balancing act in these quick-fix times. Creating purposeful work takes a combination of short-term and long-term thinking—spending time in the present and the future.

Some of us struggle with discipline. We lack patience and have trouble delaying gratification. We want it all now: the results, the money and the fame. This reminds me of the Dr. Seuss book, *Oh The Places You'll Go*, in which the main character was searching for fame, and fame he got, except when he didn't, which happened to be more often than not. Into a downhill slump he went and, of course, unslumping yourself is not easy to do.

Success, money and purposeful work without the tools and foundation to support them will all too soon crumble. We need discipline more than ever to create purposeful work in order to:

1. Stick it out in challenging times—and times are challenging
2. Focus on our agenda—when distractions are everywhere
3. Cultivate patience and determination as we create work that may go against the status quo

4. Stay balanced in the midst of change and chaos
5. Walk our talk and model our model to "be" our work!

It takes discipline to remain in the uncomfortable places where life and work are now leading us. Most people would choose to jump out of the pot and end up in the frying pan. Things are heating up.

Self-discipline originates from within. As we grow into mature adults we realize that we are the ones structuring our time and resources. You know your life and work better than anyone else. You know what you need to do next. The ramifications will impact you and others you work with. Your self-discipline or lack of it will work for or against you. The following Challenge will assist you in cultivating this important tool for your purposeful tool kit.

SELF-DISCIPLINE CHALLENGE

This new form of discipline is needed by all of us in today's ever-changing work world. Please complete the following Challenge to further build self-discipline.

Thanks so much,
Patricia

1. Review the following list of attributes of self-discipline and rate yourself relative to each. Use a scale of 1–10, with 1 being you *don't* do and 10 meaning you *always* do.

    Stick it out in the tough times   1 2 3 4 5 6 7 8 9 10

    Focus on my agenda   1 2 3 4 5 6 7 8 9 10

    Cultivate patience and determination   1 2 3 4 5 6 7 8 9 10

    Keep digging deeper to get to the core
    of any situation   1 2 3 4 5 6 7 8 9 10

Stay balanced in the midst of change
and chaos   1 2 3 4 5 6 7 8 9 10

Walk your talk, model your model,
"be" your work   1 2 3 4 5 6 7 8 9 10

2. Which area needs more focus? What can you do to build your self-
    discipline in this area?

SELF-ASSERTIVENESS

Self-assertiveness is easier to achieve after we have first integrated
the tools we have just discussed: self-awareness, self-acceptance,
self-responsibility and self-discipline. We then know how, when and
why we are choosing to be assertive—we are able to be consciously
assertive from the right context.

There is little risk in being assertive when we have first done our
homework. If we believe in ourselves, others will as well—and, of
course, the opposite is also true. When we value ourselves, our work
and our purpose, we want to openly communicate this because we
can see the value for others.

Self-assertiveness at work and within our businesses and
organizations—from a purposeful perspective—means claiming and
acting on the work world we want to create, one that brings meaning
and makes a difference. Bringing the future of work into day-to-day
reality requires assertiveness in our ideals and ideas.

There is a great parallel between being assertive and what we might
call speaking our truth—they are often one and the same. Consistently
living and working from the truth is one of the hardest positions to
take, especially in the workplace. Why? Because telling the truth,
being assertive, often goes against the grain. When approached with a

negative attitude, it can create distance and separation when the goal is just the opposite. Furthermore, some of us were taught to "follow the rules and be nice," and those old tapes are deeply grooved.

At the same time it is vital to remember what the truth can create. It can literally transform. Speaking the truth takes courage.

> *My failure to speak the truth and be assertive recently led to the demise of a working relationship. I just didn't have the courage to say what needed to be said early on, and I believe we both lost because of it. I had invited an associate to be a part of a proposal I was working on for a long-standing client. We were moving the work to the next level and I felt her work would compliment the effort. But I had reservations. I wasn't being truthful with myself or with her. I was wavering in my decision making and thus giving mixed messages. I kept mum. I realized, with a bit of surprise, that we were not moving in the direction I foresaw. Somehow the tables had turned and we were headed down a road contrary to the work model proposed. I finally had to speak up.*
>
> *What had kept me from opening my mouth earlier? My fear of offending and the thought of "who do I think I am?"—an old tape. I doubted what I recognized as true in order to keep things comfortable. Or so I thought.*

Being assertive, when used for the sake of evolution, holds great power. It creates opportunities for new feelings, thinking and ideas—even new behaviors. It's an opportunity to act on our wisdom.

Some of you may be saying, "Sounds good. Let's get started." While others may be saying, "Share my truth, my wisdom? Come on, with *my* clients?"

Being assertive demands that we understand three things well—our selves, our purpose and others that we work with. This is not a dance we dance alone, for it requires partners that are aligned with the process. Our job is to act as the guide as we follow the lead of others.

There is a readiness involved in truth-telling. The end result goes beyond win-win—it taps the higher good of all concerned. If done poorly it can feel like win-lose. It is our job to see that this doesn't happen. If we aggressively impose, then everyone loses.

Consider the following steps as practice to develop self-assertiveness. In a way, this is just good relationship building.

1st – Acquire a deep sense of self-awareness—know your work purpose.

2nd – Focus on understanding those you work with.

3rd – Determine the higher good of all concerned and make this the starting point.

4th – Put yourself in the shoes of others and speak their language.

5th – Have a goal of alignment and agreement.

6th – Collectively determine the first small step—together.

There is a great responsibility to being assertive, and this lies, I believe, with the person who is most aware. Don't get caught placing the responsibility on others and then playing the blame game. This is an escape tactic if I ever saw one—we are so good at hiding from our power. Besides, at some level, people do want to hear the truth!

SELF-ASSERTIVENESS CHALLENGE:

Please complete the following Challenge to develop the muscle of assertiveness, and we will collectively create the new world of work.

Thanks so much,
Patricia

1. Here again, we are working on a three-part sentence completion exercise. At the beginning of each day for five days come up with

6–10 endings for one of the following sentence fragments. The endings can repeat themselves.

✦ *It would help to be more self-assertive around…*

✦ *Being more self-assertive about my work/business would…*

2. Next – at the end of the five days, write 6–10 endings for one of the above statements using the following format:

   When I reflect on how I would feel if I were *(place the sentence fragment here)*, then…

3. Now, go back and reread what you have written, then write down 6–10 endings for the following:

   If any of what I wrote this week is true, it would be helpful if I…

C-3. THE DEEPER LEVELS

In this Tool we have been focusing on what it takes to develop the confidence and courage to move beyond the status quo. We have been developing the inner foundation and new strength necessary toward self-mastery.

We've focused on developing the core tools of self-awareness, self-acceptance, self-responsibility, self-discipline and self-assertiveness. As we integrate these tools, there will be a noticeable change in our lives and, of course, our work. We will become more grounded in our resolve, our purpose will become clearer and our work will become easier.

You will find that there are many by-products of these tools, all of which are beneficial. They result in yet another set of tools: **self-esteem, self-respect, self-efficacy** and **self-love**. These are the "deeper-level" tools because they are a natural result of our commitment to living and bringing the core tools into our work.

These deeper-level tools sustain us in the hard times. They let us know that we are on track and that the core tools are integrated into our daily lives and work.

SELF-ESTEEM

*"Self-esteem — the disposition to experience
oneself as being competent to cope with the basic
challenges of life and of being worthy of happiness.
To trust one's mind and to know that one is worthy
of happiness is the essence of self-esteem."*
– *"The Six Pillars of Self-Esteem"*

Self-esteem is a personal evaluation of one's life. You judge yourself as capable, competent and successful or as less than satisfactory, incompetent and unsuccessful. Our self-perception translates into how we feel, act and interact at work. If our self-esteem is high, it translates into day-to-day competence to carry out the work at hand.

Do you feel worthy of creating work that makes you happy? Are you competent to face the challenges to get there? An emphatic YES is necessary to transform work from the inside out. A no means that the core tools have not been fully developed and revisiting may be necessary.

The tools of the self, directly or indirectly obtained, are not static states of being. We often find our level of self-esteem straddling the fence between worthy of creating fulfilling work and not worthy of even the lousy job we have! This is where our state of consciousness plays such a vital role because the more conscious we are, the more it's reflected in our sense of self-esteem.

> *As I write this, I realize that I have work to do. My self-esteem can wane with the weather. It doesn't feel on solid ground. I've struggled with writing this piece, and I now realize that this is because I lack clarity around just what self-esteem is for me. I thought of it as a "feel good" feeling about oneself. But it is much more. It's an attitude and perception of worthiness of the good things in life (whatever that is for you and me) and a knowing that I deserve and am competent and capable of gaining just that.*

SELF-RESPECT

Self-respect is living your highest values, the feeling that joy and happiness are your natural birthright, and that you are good and worthwhile and deserving of the respect of others. When there is a schism between our personal ideals and how we manifest them through work, our self-respect is damaged. This slowly undermines our self-confidence until either our ideals or our work must change—I don't recommend giving up your ideals.

Our self-respect is heightened when we walk our talk, are congruent with our words and actions, and are doing what we must, even if it goes against the grain. Respect is present when we are being true to ourselves and living out our values.

Respect can be a funny thing. I believe we gain respect from others when we live up to our ideals. Often we think the opposite is true—we will lose respect. Others may not agree with you, but they will respect you. Even in the worst work situation we can do our best to live up to our standards. In fact, this type of situation often can encourage that fire in our belly that ignites us to encourage change.

As we accept and live out our values and ideals at work, we are more sensitive to respecting others' diverse values and ideals. As with all these tools, we must truly own them first to then appreciate them in others. We can be the mirrors through which others gain respect.

SELF-EFFICACY

This is our confidence in the functioning of the mind, in our ability to think, understand and learn, choose and make decisions. It is the belief in our ability to successfully take action and perform a specific behavior—to change.

What stops us is that we don't always trust our own decision making. We defer to others, constantly second-guessing ourselves, and in the end often decide not to decide. Procrastination, missed deadlines and poor results are then the output.

But if self-efficacy is present, then so is self-esteem, competence and self-respect. We then know we are making the best decision at the moment given the awareness, knowledge and resources we have to date. We believe in our decisions and thus our actions.

Through our work this is demonstrated in our ability to complete tasks with a sense of assurance of a job well done and to have confidence in change if change is needed. Self-efficacy helps us feel good about ourselves.

SELF-LOVE

Self-love is unconditional, regardless of the action or outcome. It's the ability to say "I'm great!"—not from a sense of ego or grandiosity, but from a grounded sense of self.

We're not often told we're great or to love ourselves. Therefore self-love may first take an unlearning—loosening up and letting go of self-doubt and self-reproach.

So, stop right now and embrace yourself. Give yourself a big hug—a hug of self-love. This is up to us now, for others will never be able to give you the love you need, and our wishing is never going to make it so.

Self-love, like self-respect, impacts how we see ourselves and ultimately how we see and treat others. It's rooted in a nonjudgmental perception of the world. It provides us with the mindset and behavior necessary to create purposeful work.

> *"Everyone has a price, and Life respects that price. But that price is not measured in dollars or gold, it is measured in love. And more than that, it is measured in self-love...*
> *When you love yourself, your price is very high."*
>
> *– "The Mastery of Love,"*
> *Don Miguel Ruiz*

C-3. The Deeper Levels – Here's the Challenge:

This Challenge will let you further explore self-esteem, self-respect, self-efficacy and self-love.

Sending a big hug,
Patricia

Draw and / or write about yourself demonstrating high self-esteem, self-respect, self-efficacy and self-love through your work/ business.

✦ *How are you "being" with yourself and others?*
✦ *What are you doing?*
✦ *What are your interactions like?*
✦ *Are you demonstrating a higher degree of purposefulness? If so, how?*

D. Beyond Self-Deception to Self-Realization

An ancient prophet once said, "There is no worse blind man than the one who doesn't want to see. There is no worse deaf man than the one who doesn't want to hear. There is no worse madman than the one who doesn't want to understand."

As a race, humans are the only species capable of self-deception. We fool ourselves constantly. Inevitably, this behavior plays itself out in our work environments, and because we're so good at it, we don't even see it coming. We check our coats and beliefs at the door as we play the game of politics, policies and protection. We fear the repercussions of telling the truth. Face it: we might lose a project or even our livelihood.

So we can't ignore or neglect the flip side of the tools, which comprises **self-doubt, self-denial** and **self-sabotage**. Doing so in itself is self-denial. We have learned to avoid pain and self-responsibility. We can't be responsible for what we don't know about ourselves, right? Wrong.

We can't develop a personal asset or use it toward a greater good if we deny its existence. Nor can we choose to recognize a personal liability if we constantly rationalize its presence. We see what we want, what we can handle at the moment. What we don't see sabotages us. It will sneak up when we least expect it and bite us in the foot.

We all have strengths and weaknesses, assets and liabilities, and in the end a purpose. Often that purpose can be daunting. But we can no longer afford to be in self-doubt or self-denial about it. Work that makes a difference and impacts the lives of many is needed now more than ever, given the current chaotic state of world in general.

I recently realized that I was blaming God for my life and business not going as I wanted. I thought since I was doing work for the greater good that the work would just happen—somehow. I thought if I put the word out on creating purposeful work that people would come—"Field of Dreams" wishful thinking. I'm not saying that this can't happen, but my ego had a vested interest in its happening. I had huge expectations and felt entitled. Self-sabotage, if I ever saw it. I was playing the victim of my own creation—a very hard lesson, to be sure.

We have learned, very tactfully, to use a false sense of strength to keep us from seeing our truth. We have manipulated life in order to stay in denial and play safe. Little do we know that the truth denied will work against us. It can sabotage our very lives, preventing us from being our authentic selves, living out our purpose and ultimately getting what we want most. Only truth will give us the freedom we so desire.

SELF-DOUBT

When in self-doubt, we second-guess our decision-making and discount what we know to be true. The scenario goes this way: we doubt ourselves, lack confidence and then hide out in work for which we're over-qualified. We work with individuals who reinforce our self-doubt, who make excuses for our poor behavior, and then we don't expect too much of ourselves.

Self-doubt is rooted in a lack of self-awareness and self-confidence. We lack the grounding and reference point of self. Our internal check-and-balance system is missing and we have little to believe in. We end up knowing only the distorted personality side of ourselves and not our essence.

Overcoming self-doubt requires a belief and trust in our opinions, perspective, knowledge and wisdom. It's a gradual building of new internal reference points. These reference points will then guide us toward what is right for us.

*"For the optimal realization of our work possibilities, we
need to admire ourselves and trust ourselves, and the
trust and admiration needs to be grounded in reality, not
generated out of fantasy and self-delusion. I can project an
image of assurance and poise that fools almost everyone
and yet secretly tremble with a sense of my inadequacy."*
— "The Six Pillars of Self-Esteem"

SELF-DENIAL

Self-denial is to sacrifice our own desires or pleasures. This is
commonplace in the work world when fear is the motivator. We
become solely focused on our security, financial or otherwise. We in
turn sell out, give away what we want most in life and deny our very
selves.

We say it doesn't matter, and we rationalize the situation to make
ourselves and others comfortable. We convince ourselves that it's OK.
Well it's not!

We follow the agenda placed on us by either not having one of our
own or putting ours second place. If we don't have the power or the
sanction, we need to give ourselves permission to take it. That's right.
This is where the rubber meets the road. It's time to conjure up the
courage and rely on your newly heightened skills of self-confidence
and self-assertiveness to come into play. We all know what we must
do, and it's time to do it.

SELF-SABOTAGE

When we do this, we unwittingly work against ourselves. Self-
sabotage occurs as an unconscious action. We don't see it
coming, it sneaks up on us and we pay a high price. Only when we
are willing to face what's behind these destructive actions, when we
are in enough pain or have enough passion, will we see the truth.

Self-sabotage happens when we aren't quite ready to come face-to-face with our fears. We must tackle many layers of denial before we are willing to see the core of the sabotaging belief and behavior.

Overcoming self-sabotaging behaviors takes admitting that we always play a role in all situations. If we don't like the results we are getting, then we only need to look at ourselves. This is sometimes very hard for us to admit because we usually prefer to blame. We blame others, the situation, the economy, our upbringing—anything and anyone in order to not examine ourselves. In fact, it is not about blame but about responsibility. Our responsibility to our selves, our lives, our happiness and our own evolution demands self-examination.

If we choose to recognize and come to terms with our sabotaging shadow-side. We will see a side of ourselves that we may not like but need to live with. We need to shake hands will our whole self, which of course includes the self that is stubborn, selfish, immature, etc. No shortage of recognition for us here.

We can learn to get out of our own way if we can embrace—not ignore—our ability to be in self-doubt, self-denial and self-sabotage. If we can catch them as they surface, then we can consciously choose to reroute our behavior. It now becomes a proactive choice not just reactive response. The result is a healthier, more sustainable life and work.

D. BEYOND SELF-DECEPTION TO SELF-REALIZATION – HERE'S THE CHALLENGE:

Please complete the following Challenge exercises to further explore self-doubt, self-denial and self-sabotage.

You have come far,
Patricia

1. How do you know when you are fooling yourself into believing something that isn't the "truth of reality"? Does anger or judgment show its ugly head? Explain.

2. What do you know is true about you—the positive and the negative—that you sometimes deny? Think in terms of the self-sabotaging shadow-side of self. Then state the reason you deny these attributes.

The truth about myself:	Why I might be denying this:

3. Write about an unpleasant or unsuccessful situation at work or within your business. What part did you play in contributing to this situation? In what way could a self-sabotaging behavior have prevented a positive outcome? Now take a few minutes to reflect on and write about what you could have done differently.

TOOL 4

FEAR AS AN ALLY

A. *Worst Enemy/Best Friend*

B. *Don't Fear What You Want Most*

C. *Embracing Your Resistance*

D. *Fear Is Love in Disguise*

A. Worst Enemy/Best Friend

*"The true value of a human being can be found in the
degree to which he has attained liberation from the self."*
– Albert Einstein

As many of you know, love and fear cannot coexist. This holds true in all areas of our lives, and work/business is no exception. We operate either from a state of love or from a state of fear. In the workplace today, fear still dominates as the primary motivator. This is rather astonishing given the well-educated and well-off society we live in. In times past, when most were illiterate and poor as paupers, one could understand. But now it almost seems incomprehensible. It just seems so backwards.

Production is up because fear of losing one's job or business has increased. People are working extraordinary hours because they think they are dispensable. In some cases they are. They are walking a very thin line, afraid to rock the boat, concerned about upsetting the Boss, Client, Stockholders or Board. Small businesses are doing whatever they can to keep themselves afloat, taking projects outside their scope and vision. Their current work or business mindset has them trapped. They often wonder why they are doing this work in the first place.

There is little time to reflect, strategically plan the next step or, heaven forbid, make a mistake and learn in the process. Making a living still takes precedence over creating a life.

Many jobs are gone for good. They have been outsourced to Mexico, China, India and wherever else there is "cheaper" labor. I see this as an opportunity, not a problem. But the opportunity will surface only when we leverage our unique skills and create a "higher" level of work. But the predominance of fear is even preventing *this* from happening.

Fear has been said to be the natural reaction to change. I disagree. Fear is and has always been a learned response. Society has taught us fear, and we have learned it well. Fear represses, makes us believe—or hope—that others or some external force will save the day. We acquiesce to what the economy is doing, where the competition is, what clients will buy and the next barking order from our boss or client. We rarely stop to examine how we the individual and we the business might be the solution to this very challenge.

We are looking in the wrong direction. The answers are right in front of us—or should I say *are* **us**. Meaning me, you, your business partners, your coworkers, your employees, your Board members and anyone else associated with your work or business. The answers are literally and figuratively at our fingertips.

Uncovering these answers will demand changes we may have never faced before. We need to befriend ourselves, our knowledge, our love and our wisdom. These latter two are the source and the key to the next revolution of work. Without this shift there is little chance of evolving into what we are meant to be and do in our lifetime.

The opportunity for self-actualization is before us. Do we take the risk and change what we can, or do we continue to play it small and safe? Will we further reinforce the codependent work world, or will we evolve into the inter-independent work world many of us want?

Hasn't fear kept us in our place long enough? Since we are the only ones we can change, let's each do our part. That way we are the hero or heroine of our story, work and world. Time is running out! Our future and THE future are at stake. The next work/business revolution is in our hands.

A. Worst Enemy/Best Friend – Here's the <u>Challenge</u>:

It's difficult to face our own fears because of the pain that surfaces. This Challenge section is hard but well worth the effort. Give yourself about 20 minutes or more. If your answers don't immediately surface, come back later. Do finish this exercise before moving forward.

Thank you so much,
Patricia

1. In your work/business, where does fear have you by the throat? Where are you holding back and stuck? Why?

2. How would your work story read if you had no fear? Write it now.

B. Don't Fear What You Want Most

So how do we get beyond this cycle of fear? We need to first and foremost see fear for what it really is: a great teacher. If we see it as such, there is much to learn.

Fears exist on many levels. Some see exploring their fears as peeling an onion. I see it more as opening doors to the self. These doors are portals into a greater understanding of our true depth. This journey is difficult, so it's best to keep the end goal in mind.

Fear is our resistance to our own truth. If we see the truth and act on it appropriately, there is freedom. If we don't want to face the truth, then fear surfaces, and we are in pain. Instead of interpreting pain as a signal to shift a perception, we see it as a signal to resist.

This perception of fear as a teacher is not common. It doesn't fit any of our current thought patterns on what fear is; therefore, our mind may create confusion and doubt. For now, try to let the struggle go and continue reading.

In order to gain a broad perspective, let's step back and examine fear, digging down three levels to three portals. Let's start with the short list.

Door Number One:
The Typical Fears That Surface in the Workplace

We call it fear of change or the unknown. We are stopped in our tracks from the very beginning. We often aren't even willing to talk about the fear to identify its cause. We think staying innocent will keep us safe. Instead, we remain stuck until we are willing to dig deeper.

As soon as fear starts showing its face, the paradox begins. We think we are afraid of the following when sometimes we are afraid of the exact opposite.

The Short List of Fears

✦ *Change itself and the unknown behind it*

✦ *Standing up for our rights, wants and needs and the conflict that might surface*

✦ *Expressing emotions and feelings—being vulnerable at work*

✦ *Taking on a greater level of responsibility*

✦ *A downgrade of status*

✦ *Having the "hard," truthful conversations*

✦ *Loss—of power, respect, acceptance, money, etc.*

✦ *Gain—of power, respect, acceptance, money, etc.*

(These last two would be laughable if they weren't so true.)

Our reply to this list, on an unconscious level, might be "Darn right! I don't want to lose my financial security"; "I'm not going to let my guard down"; "I don't trust that person"; or "I don't want that added responsibility." Then again, our response might be none of these, and denial may have the upper hand. Think about it!

Fear is the modus operandi of the unconscious mind, and it will do anything to hold onto this existence. Change is out—rationalization is in. If this doesn't provide enough fuel to maintain the fear, then the external world surely will. This is part of the dance. The question is, Who's leading?

This is the beginning and the first cause to win. It's the tip of the iceberg, where many of us get stuck and close the door. The *yes-but, if-only* and *what-if* keep us on the surface.

Door Number Two: A Subsequent, Much Deeper Fear

We are afraid of what we want most in life. We fear having it all, however *all* is defined. Afraid of greater happiness, success, wealth, wisdom, health, true partnership, purposeful work—you name yours. This list is a long one.

We often fear what having it all will ask of us in return. Could we handle this? Do we even want to?

Having it all means moving beyond small. It requires us to broaden our perspective of self and work; be more self-aware, responsible and disciplined; and face our fears. It also means encountering and acting on numerous levels of change—first within ourselves.

This challenging process will surface yet greater fears. Is the known fear easier to handle than the unknown, even if the result is having it all? It's like the saying "The devil we know is better than the devil we don't!" But not if we're selling ourselves out in the process.

I don't need to go any further than myself on this one. This strikes home for me. On one level I know I can and will have it all, but the fear side says "Do I deserve it?" Subconscious mind chatter is having its day.

To me, having it all means: a global business that does nothing less than evolve our perspective of self and work; wonderful supportive partners; all the money I need; a true partner; a community of like-minded individuals; a beautiful home; joy and inner peace; and a kinder, gentler work world that is an incubator for evolving the human spirit.

This is the world I want for myself and others who have this desire. This is the world I long to live in. It will happen as I do the work of learning from fear and, in turn, gain freedom. It is a world waiting to happen.

The world you want may be different than mine, but I have no doubt that at the core many similarities exist. Otherwise, you wouldn't be reading this book. You also have a list of what you want most.

Door Number Three: The Ultimate Fear We Face

Transcendence and Self-actualization—the ultimate human needs and, oddly enough, potentially the greatest fear. The thought of reaching self-actualization and eventually helping others to do the same can be difficult to comprehend because so few have reached these levels. The evolution to these states can be either extremely frightening or exceptionally encouraging.

The pinnacle is our *need* to be all that we can be. If we fear having it all, we certainly fear being it all. We have few role models. We don't know how to even think about this, let alone create a supportive belief system. Getting to this state will require a tremendous foundation of self-awareness, self-love and self-responsibility.

Along the evolutionary way, self-sabotage will surface. We limit ourselves from the very beginning. We live in our narrow assumptions, limiting boundaries and negative beliefs. These keep us in outdated stories of our lives and work. We attract others with the same story to feel secure—saved yet again.

As a species, we fight our own beingness, our true nature. We don't see the rabbit, elephant, fly or hawk betraying itself. They all know their power and vulnerabilities and live accordingly. They bring all of themselves into the world each day. Their life and work are congruent. They suffer no inner conflict. They are bold, playful, strong and powerful. Are we?

In the work world, the fear of our true nature is a detriment to what our work often needs most. That is for us to operate from our highest potential and deepest humanity. The workplace desperately needs these deeper aspects of self if it is to serve people, profits and the planet and survive in these complex business times.

If WE began today to take one step toward operating at a higher level, the outcome would be startling. We would:

+ *Take off our masks and allow our humanness and vulnerability to surface.*
+ *Tap into a deeper level of wisdom to address the problems we face.*

✦ *More consciously monitor our actions, knowing that everything has a consequence in the collective global sense. We would act to preserve, not destroy.*

✦ *Realize that we need to operate at two levels: one of human spirit and the other of profitable entity.*

Humans misuse their minds. In its unconscious state the mind has become the reservoir of fear. Only its conscious state will allow us to create the above, and this can happen only if we surrender to our true nature.

In the end the request is simple: Be Human. Be your true self and stop fighting it. This job of being human is naturally ours to do. We possess all that we need. We can create the life and work of our choice.

> *"And will you succeed? Yes! You will indeed!*
> *(98 and 3/4 percent guaranteed.)*
> *KID, YOU'LL MOVE MOUNTAINS!"*
> *– Dr. Seuss*

Your internal mountain is waiting. The external rewards will come in due time. Evolution does need our cooperation, for the clock is ticking. So watch out when it's time—nothing will stop you. Guaranteed!

B. Don't Fear What You Want Most – Here's the <u>Challenge</u>:

Give yourself plenty of time to complete the following Challenge. Don't let fear get in your way.

Thanks for your strength,
Patricia

1. Door Number One: What inevitable change are you facing in your work/business that you are most apprehensive about? What one thing can you do to act on this concern?

2. Door Number Two: What do you want most concerning your work? What internally generated fear(s) might be preventing this from happening?

3. Door Number Three: Relative to self-actualization and transcendence, where do you find yourself? How can you "be" different to consistently live at higher levels?

C. Embracing Your Resistance

The writing is on the wall and the clock is ticking. Fear in the form of complacency, protectionism and false security is dividing our head and heart.

We can learn much by identifying and shaking hands with our fears. With transcendence as our end goal, we have much to do.

But we get easily sidetracked. We convince ourselves that everything is fine. We...

1. Rationalize our fear: "I'm exactly where I want to be. This work is great." (Even though behind the scenes we are dying on the vine.)
2. Reinforce fear: "The market is tough, and I'm just glad I have this business." (We make a case for playing small.)
3. Deny fear: "I'm not concerned about making this change. I can do this any time I want." (The truth is we are so scared we don't do anything.)

I've been there many times. I've given every reason possible to run from myself. Fear, old limiting beliefs and my unconscious have been pulling the strings.

This time I can't let fear win—the dance has gone on for too long. I'm up against the highest wall yet. I give up and surrender yet again. I need to remember that giving up does not mean giving in. Giving in would be compromising my values and soul. Giving up, however, means letting go of the control—not something I easily do.

I've paid a dear price for stuffing my fear. This has left me with physical, emotional and financial pain. I can't afford to hold onto this any longer.

Since I operate knowing that all actions impact the larger whole, releasing this fear will affect more than me. It will help loosen the larger generational pull to the past that maintains the dysfunctional status quo. It sometimes feels like the past has a hold on my mind, my emotions, and every cell of my body and keeps pulling me back into my small self. I can no longer run from myself.

Fear and pain are knocking at our door to be embraced, not run from. They come bringing gifts.

When we stand our ground we are like a tree in a strong wind that

EVOLUTIONARY WORK CASE STUDY

MICHAEL
Purposeful Business Circle Member

I find that the Purposeful Business Circle helps me keep moving my business in the direction of living with an open heart. It is easy when involved in the day-to-day details of running a business to forget why you started it and the bigger picture. Sometimes when things are going right, fear and other negative emotions can take over. The Circle helps me to keep moving my business in a more spiritually satisfying direction while still focusing on getting the important things done in a relaxed way.

During the Circle, Patricia encourages us to learn from each other and write down action steps to work on for the next two months. We then check in three times on these steps: once with a buddy, once on teleconference call and then at the next full Circle meeting. I find this checking in and cheering from other members helps me to keep doing the tasks that I want to do but that are easy to put off for more urgent day-to-day tasks.

In the three years since I joined the Circle I am now calm and focused when outside changes occur. Whereas, before I would be depressed and tend to withdraw emotionally from my business when a crisis happened. While the crises still occur, I flow through or around them.

bends but doesn't break. We return to center with a renewed strength. The time is now for our greater selves and work to stand strong.

Know that fear is a false god rooted in misdirected security needs. We have been willing participants and enforcers in this game of playing small.

> "The
> Difference
> Between a good artist
> And a great one
> Is:
> The novice
> Will often lay down his tool
> Or brush
> Then pick up an invisible club
> On the mind's table
> And helplessly smash the easels and
> Jade.
> Whereas the vintage man
> No longer hurts himself or anyone
> And keeps on
> Sculpting
> Light"
>
> – "The Vintage Man,"
> Hafiz, The Great Sufi Master

C. Embracing Your Resistance – Here's the Challenge

Over the many years of doing this work with my clients and myself, I've had many opportunities to use the following exercises. They have always worked. Below you will find the first two steps of a five-step process of identifying and embracing our "wall of resistance." (Steps three to five are in the next section.) Give yourself plenty of time and patience to finish these.

I so appreciate your effort,
Patricia

Step One: The first thing to do is bring form to your fear. This will make it more tangible and break down its illusionary state. When fear takes more of a concrete form, you gain clarity on what you are up against.

You can draw, sculpt, use wooden blocks or even TinkerToys to give fear a recognizable form. When prompted, fear will show its face. Strange as it may seem, fear wants to help you.

To help you get started, examples from courageous clients are cited below. As you will see, fear can look like whatever it needs to for your learning, like being…

1. In a rickety old car on a very bumpy road. Ahead is a mountain that's impossible to traverse—especially in this car. It's dark, cloudy, and a storm is afoot. (Alone and lonely, you are the head of a fledgling small business, with seemingly no one to confide in.)

2. Trapped in the tallest tower of an ancient castle. In the moat below there are deadly crocodiles awaiting their prey. There is little food left, and your water is almost gone. (You need to make some grave

decisions about your work with what appear to be few viable solutions.)

3. In a suit of armor with a sword in one hand and a shield in the other. You are ready for the daily battle at work. The warriors you have to face are mighty and strong and seem to outwit you every time. (You are exhausted from this warrior stance with what seems to be no escape.)

Your turn! Take a few deep breaths, then close your eyes and focus on what you fear most, on what causes you great anxiety and pain around your work. Imagine this fear.

Next put into form whatever surfaces. Know that the image will expand as you make it more concrete. Time is ripe to start now. Bring form to your wall of resistance.

Step Two: The next thing you need to do is shift your perception of fear. What you are afraid of is not the enemy; it's your interpretation of it. The following is a three-part sentence completion exercise to spark this internal shift.

1st – Write endings to the following sentence fragment as quickly as you can. Write no fewer than six and no more than ten. Don't think; just write.

If I knew that fear had something vital to teach me, I would…

2nd – At the end of the day, write six to ten endings for the above using the following format:

When I reflect on how I would feel if I knew that fear had something vital to teach me, then…

3rd – Then go back and reread what you have written. Write down six to ten endings for the following:

If any of what I wrote is true, it would be helpful if I…

D. FEAR IS LOVE IN DISGUISE

"But you see, Meg, just because we don't understand
doesn't mean that the explanation doesn't exist."
– "A Wrinkle in Time," Madeleine L'Engle

The following perspective on fear surfaced as I was writing this section. I didn't expect it, so it may appear contrary to what I've said so far. We all have a lot to learn.

Fear is a signal to step back, look within the current situation, observe the truth and then take appropriate action. Fear is not saying stop. It is asking us to stand up for what we believe, hold on to what we know is true from the depth of our souls, build the strength needed and stop running from ourselves!

We do have the answers to make our work more purposeful, create healthy work environments and make the impact we want. Fear is not there to keep us small and safe but to lift us up and give us strength. Fear is one of our greatest friends because it won't let us get away with being any less than we are.

There are two sides to fear. It has a yin and a yang like everything else. The yang is what we usually encounter: the strong and forceful side of fear. The yin is apparent only when we stand our ground. At that point, fear transmutes to the softer, accepting side where we can find nurturing.

We would do well to embrace this new mindset concerning fear. If we do, the result will be a new behavior pattern that:

1. Doesn't acquiesce but steps into fear;
2. Knows that our dreams and desires for a new work world are more powerful than our fears around lost security, status or money;
3. Lets fear express itself—it also has wants and needs;
4. Knows it will push all our buttons, but we don't need to react;

5. Understands that this is a test to make you stronger;
6. Develops a new strength to have as an ally; and
7. Is clear that fear is here to help.

As we begin to see that fear is the direct opposite of what we think, a new world view becomes available. We might eventually learn to welcome fear, even call it forth and say "bring it on," knowing that strength, peace and freedom are on the other side—knowing that fear is love in disguise.

Given that this "new" view of fear is contrary to our current thinking, it may take time to understand and digest. We don't live in a world that recognizes fear as a friend, but that doesn't mean this is not the truth.

Knowing that we are supported every step of the way is not always easy to accept—especially when it comes to fear. Fear is here to lighten our burden and offer us a new sense of freedom. Everything is a lesson and a teacher, fear being one of our greatest.

D. FEAR IS LOVE IN DISGUISE – HERE'S THE CHALLENGE

Hopefully we can now begin to see that fear is a partner in this evolutionary process. What follows are steps three to five in our process of identifying and embracing our wall of resistance. This Challenge will allow you to see all the gifts that fear has to offer.

I appreciate all the work you are doing,
Patricia

Step Three: With fear as a friend and teacher, you can learn from what surfaced in Step One. What is your fear telling you? What is there to learn? Just ask, then listen! Write down what you hear or sense. Use single words or sentences. (What follows is based on the previous examples.)

1. The rickety old car image might be saying that your perception of work is outdated, and this old road is a rocky one indeed. It will not lead you to a new work future, but give you more of the same.

2. Being trapped in a tower could be suggesting that you come down to earth, take the first small step, make some changes, take a risk, get out of your head, try something new.

3. The suit of armor with sword and shield might be saying to ease up at work. Literally get out of your "suit," begin to see work as a place to make a difference, not fight a battle.

Step Four: This next step is very powerful. It's about giving form to your work/business situation beyond the fear. Think of yourself on the other side of the wall, beyond the barrier or outside of the boundary.

What is your work world now like? Given the lessons you've learned, what is now possible? With you and fear working together, the sky's the limit.

This step will give you insights into the direction for your new work future. Now write and draw what is on the other side of fear. (Again these examples follow from the previous.)

1. The rickety old car is transformed into an up-to-date model, traveling on a much smoother road. The bumps are fewer and far between. The sun is out, and a rainbow is guiding your way. (You realize a change is needed from the inside out.)

2. Trapped in a tower might turn into a Rumpelstiltskin story of sorts, where you make a ladder out of sheets and out the window you go. The crocodile's tame and calm. (You know that to be on solid ground you must be creative, take action and move forward.)

3. All of a sudden, there are snaps on the suit and you easily get out. You find yourself in comfortable clothes with a relaxed attitude and approach to work. You are befriending and collaborating with others. (You understand that it is up to you to take the first new step.)

Step Five: Now that you are on the other side of fear with a renewed view of work, you can entertain new behaviors. You can focus one day at a time and operate based on conscious decisions—no longer tainted by fear. How will you "be" different, and what will you "do" differently? Write your responses below.

1.
2.
3. Now, TAKE ACTION!

TOOL 5

WISDOM AS THE NEXT EVOLUTIONARY LEAP

A. *Your Intellect Is Passé*

B. *Trusting Yourself to Tell the Truth*

C. *It Is Our Work to Be Wise*

D. *Defining & Developing Wisdom*

E. *The Wisdom-Centered Visionary*™

Writing the following has raked me over the coals. I focused on what I thought most of us have access to: our internal resources of intellect, heart and intuition. What I didn't count on was that spirit had its own plans that led to an even deeper, less cultivated place, aching to surface—a place of self-love, emotional and bodily awareness, and wisdom. It was asking me not only to think different but to be different, to remember who I am in this world. I had forgotten.

I realized I needed to step back and take better care of myself at a deeper level. I had been giving away my energy and my spirit by not standing up for the work world I wanted. I was still playing too small.

I had lost all my joy. I had forgotten the necessity, not just benefit, of consistent meditation, body work and nutrition.

Through writing this Tool, I've become a more congruent, human/spiritual being. I've traveled from knowledge to integration to living differently—an often quantum leap. Now I, more than not, state my truth, wants and needs directly; act as the leader I am; and have more faith and trust in the world I long to create. I am living my convictions, not just talking about them.

This newly awakened being that many of us are evolving into knows that all thoughts and actions make a difference that ripples across the globe. This Tool will challenge you. Give it time. I hope your learning is tough enough to teach you how to remember yourself.

The poet John Berryman, in singing the praises of ordeal, says: "Among the greatest pieces of luck for high achievement is ordeal. I hope to be nearly crucified."

A. Your Intellect Is Passé

"The mind is the most valuable thing in the world.
But the deluded mind can be the most dangerous."
– His Holiness the Dalai Lama

Unlocking our purpose and creating new work/business requires wholly new thinking. Often current thinking and mindset reject rather than embrace the new. The focus is often on outer-referencing to the neglect of inner truth; constant comparison; self-protection; and more. We sell ourselves short.

When evaluating the viability of new work ideas, the old mind will say: "Unrealistic, impractical, unprofitable." With the ego as its companion, the mind has a stake in maintaining the status quo and in "looking good" for the outer world. We don't want to look like we don't know what we are doing or that we aren't in control.

We hold onto our perspective of reality, making decisions from the intellect and the wallet, ignoring the truly vital aspects of our selves that are the source of newness. We say we are spiritual individuals, but when the rubber hits the road, we are challenged indeed. We want change and new work but aren't willing to alter our lifestyle, learn new habits, or do anything that threatens our identity. In actuality, we need to do all three.

We want answers that justify our position—regardless of the higher good of self or others. Is this not ego gratification at its most seductive? We give our intellect permission to keep us in the dark so we can support our small self in words and actions.

We need to heed Einstein's words: "We can't get new answers to problems from the same level of thinking that the answers were created from in the first place." But we also need to take this a step further, from thinking to a new level of being.

In this fast-paced world, I sometimes forget that the wind talks to me and comforts me when I'm stressed, that feathers come to me as a sign that I'm on the right path, that meditation provides me with both great insight and great peace. I often need to be reminded that living from my spiritual side grants me much knowing and wisdom.

I remember now that I am precious and gifted. We all are. As the instrument of a new work world, I can "be" that world. I can be true to myself and not settle for second best.

I have just passed through another wall with new lessons and blessings on the other side. My intellect has been my master for these many years, and that is changing. My body and spirit are stepping forth. My mind wants its old ways, but my heart sings louder than ever.

For the greater good, we must all face our nemeses. We can't afford to backtrack. We need to evolve, not de-volve, and do our part.

A. Your Intellect Is Passé – Here's the <u>Challenge</u>:

Being honest with ourselves is not easy. Our small minds have such a vested interest in the way things are. I ask you to please be brutally honest with yourself here. Allow at least 20 minutes of quiet time to do the following exercises. If your answers don't immediately surface, come back later.

Thank you for digging deep—your answers are waiting to surface,
Patricia

1. How does your mind react when there is great change afoot? Answer this question in a paragraph or two, as if you were talking to yourself or a friend.

2. How might you need to reframe your thinking around the following? Creating a new work future demands more holistic, positive and proactive ways of seeing life and work. Redefine as many of the following as apply. Feel free to add to this list.

   1) Money is...
   2) Security is...
   3) Work is...
   4) Safety is...
   5) Lifestyle is...
   6)
   7)
   8)
   9)

B. Trusting Yourself
to Tell the Truth

Our bodies and emotions hold a much deeper knowing than our intellect. They operate from a truer sense of self and a greater whole. They are attuned to the bigger picture and the core issue. They bring new insight to any challenge—life and work.

Every part of us has answers to share and lessons to teach. Our cells hold memories that can hold us back or encourage us forward; our muscles react by tensing and relaxing to provide signals of stress or openness; and our organs process life physically *and* emotionally, each with its own purpose. My recurring problem with a stiff back is a signal for me to be more flexible, just as losing one's voice may be about speaking up more powerfully.

How is your body feeling right now? Where is there tension or soreness? What emotions are on the surface, so close but seemingly so far away? We don't ask ourselves these types of questions every day. They certainly don't come into play as we work to address business decisions. But they are vital if we are to achieve deeper, truer answers.

As I mentioned earlier, this Tool has been the hardest one yet to write. Not because the writing doesn't flow or because time is short, but because the inner work has been so difficult. Being the student first, I know it can be no other way. I must be the work I teach—or at least be on the path.

So as I listen to my body and my emotions I have slowed my pace. My body has been telling me to move more, spend less time at my desk and claim my sense of rhythm. Now I often stand while I work, go for more walks, have music playing most of the time and even have gone back to dancing.

In turn, my emotions have been opening up a well of long-repressed tears. I allow myself to be whatever emotion surfaces—more often than not. It's all OK—the anger, delight, sadness…the love. I'm expressing my truth and am taking better care of myself—self-love has slowly started to kick in.

EVOLUTIONARY WORK CASE STUDY

DOUG NELSON
Coaching Client

Through this work I'm connecting with my self and the world in ways that I never have before. I have always had a strong sense of purpose, but I had a very difficult time expressing it in any practical way. I knew my life's work was important, and the inability to express it was stagnating. This work helped me to dissolve limiting beliefs and bridge the gap between my potential and the expression of it in the world.

Working with Patricia is a form of enlightened partnership. I always have a deep sense of gratitude for the light she is able to bring to our work together, and at the same time I am that much more aware of how I shine. In hour-long conversations she would accurately pinpoint the most pressing issues and would help to establish action steps. Initially, I dreaded these as it inevitably meant walking directly and methodically into my blind spots. Now I find I look forward to addressing action steps because I know from experience how freeing it is.

Creating artwork has always been a sacred process for me. It's a form of meditation and a spiritual tool that I use to explore and expand my reality. Art is the most visible expression of my life's work, but it's only recently that I have been able offer it to anyone else in a practical way. About a year ago, as one of the action steps I began sharing images of recent work via email to a small group of people. I immediately felt a surge in creativity simply knowing the images were being received. I have sent out images weekly since then, and the mailing list has grown to 76 people. I had a significant show three months ago where 12 paintings, 1/3 of the show, sold opening night. I am currently showing work on a semi-permanent basis in three different venues. The structure that I'm building around art as business, largely out of action steps, is simple, flexible, profitable and infinitely practical.

Katherine Woodward Thomas, in her book *Calling in The One*, speaks of creating emotional literacy, which she defines as "the ability to accurately read one's own feelings, to manage them by self-soothing or delaying impulsivity to some extent and then to comprehend and respond appropriately to the feelings of others." She goes on to call emotional literacy the "currency" of all relationships.

As we move into the "social relationship" orientation of work, the more important emotional literacy becomes. We can now begin to see that money is only one of many types of currencies in the workplace. Besides our emotions, we can add our hearts, intuition and bodily sensations to this list. We can even go as far as to say that using these inner resources provides an added value to any work situation.

We need to have a conversation with our aches and pains, as well as listen to our emotions. Developing this skill takes time. It is not the quick fix that many are after. It demands a slower pace, a letting go.

Without this more holistic approach, we will continue to play on the surface, to conduct business as usual. We often avoid working toward this next level of truth. If we don't evolve this inside-out approach to work, then command-and-control will continue to rule.

"This is a journey that we are all on, everybody on the planet, whether we like it or not; whether we know it or not; whether it is unfolding according to plan or not. Life is what it is about, and the challenge of living it as if it really mattered. Being human, we always have a choice in this regard. We can either be passively carried along by forces and habits that remain stubbornly unexamined and which imprison us in distorted dreams and potential nightmares, or we can engage our lives by waking up to them and participating fully in their unfolding, whether we "like" what is happening in any moment or not. Only when we wake up do our lives become real and have a chance of being liberated from our individual and collective delusions, diseases and suffering."

– "Coming to Our Senses: Healing Ourselves and the World Through Mindfulness,"
Jon Kabat-Zinn

B. TRUSTING YOURSELF TO TELL THE TRUTH – HERE'S THE <u>CHALLENGE</u>:

Trusting our whole selves takes practice. Please answer and act on the following exercises. New insights are guaranteed.

Thank you so much,
Patricia

1. How do you make decisions? Take time to focus and give this thought. Check off as many as apply, and add your own to the list. After you're finished, write down which of the following you aren't doing that would be of value. Write why and how they would bring value.

    a. *Explore what is most practical* ___
    b. *Listen to my intuition* ___
    c. *Sense what my body is telling me* ___
    d. *Explore my feelings around the issue* ___
    e. *Do what I feel others expect of me* ___
    f. *Write or journal on the subject* ___
    g. *Ask my heart for its reply* ___
    h.
    i.

2. What is your body telling you right now? Is there any discomfort? If so, where? Is your back saying, "take a break and relax," or your queasy stomach saying, "calm down, breathe, all is OK"? Focus on your body. Ask any painful parts what they need to tell you. Write down the responses. Then take action.

3. Emotionally, what are you feeling right now? Are you feeling happy, angry, sad, fearful or something else? Sit with this feeling for a few minutes—don't push it away. What is this telling you?

C. It Is Our Work to Be Wise

"In pursuit of knowledge, every day something is acquired.
In pursuit of wisdom, every day something is dropped."
– Lao Tzu

In these times of uncertainty at every corner, where tomorrow can change on a dime, our sense of self and work is constantly being challenged. Our work world today is like a moving target, full of unknowns.

When we play on the surface, we park our values, not to mention our wisdom, at the door as we walk into our places of work/business. We aim for the quick fix, not the long-lasting solution. We waste valuable time on the same old problems and patterns, where ignorance holds us prisoner to repeating the past instead of evolving into a new future.

Devoid of wisdom, we spin backwards. Our current problem solving does not suffice. These answers are now too small, limited in depth and breadth, and unable to create sustainable results. We are blocked from evolving into a new mental model of work that is more inclusive, inter-independent and wise.

The evolution of work will happen when these outdated patterns are transformed. Only then will we find new middle-ground, centered and functioning from wisdom and sustainable for the long-term. When we tap this, the work world will forever be changed

As we evolve through the Seven Evolutionary Tools and stages of Maslow's Hierarchy of Needs, the work world naturally follows suit. There are parallel ladders (see the diagram on the next page). The Industrial Revolution is at the lowest point but still alive and kicking in many corporate boardrooms; the Technology Revolution is an ongoing state, providing us with the tools of global connection; Knowledge and Social Relationship Management are allowing us to now realize what matters most: people. Today's enlivened workplace sits here. This focus on people as the core of work is developing into new work models that tap and leverage human potential. However, the enlightened workplace knows there is further to go—as there always is—for wisdom is what is needed to truly address broader and deeper human needs—to truly evolve. The complex problems of today can be solved only from a new "beingness," which operates from wisdom and the tapping of universal knowledge available to all.

The Evolution of Work

+ *Wisdom Development*
+ *Social Relationship Management*
+ *Knowledge Management*
+ *Technology Revolution*
+ *Industrial Revolution*

Our work is to bring our wisdom into the world on a daily basis and a grand scale. Wisdom sits at the tip of our tongue, longing to be spoken. We have the answers—YOU have the answers.

When people are speaking and acting from wisdom, what they say hits a core of truth as we nod in recognition. Too often we fail to recognize and acknowledge our own wisdom. This "not knowing," along with not trusting, prevents us from acknowledging the wisdom within. We shy away from demonstrating it, as if it's too grand an attribute to possess. We are no longer the common person when wisdom is at play. We fear the position it puts us in. That old voice echoes, "Who do you think you are?" It stops us in our tracks.

We've been running from what we know needs to evolve long enough. With wisdom at the core of our work, we can develop work models that will meet deeper human needs: connection, healing, love, growth and development—evolution itself. This new realm of business is the one many of us seek—one that feeds the pocketbook as well as the soul.

C. It Is Our Work to Be Wise –
Here's the **Challenge**:

I must say it again: YOU are wise. The key is to trust yourself and your knowing enough to bring wisdom out through your work. The following exercises will help you to step back to see and act on this.

As always, give yourself time to do the following,
Patricia

1. First, list the outdated attributes you see lingering in your place of work that limit wisdom. These attributes are often based in protectionism, fear, lack, distrust, control, power over, linear thinking, limited bottom-line focus, hierarchy and/or paternalism. Then list the contrasting "evolved" attributes that encourage wisdom.

   Add to the following list based on what you perceive:

De volved Work Model		Evolved Work Model
Exclusion	*or*	*Inclusion*
Distrust	*or*	*Trust*
Holding onto power	*or*	*Sharing power*

2. The harder task is to identify and list the outdated, de-volving attributes or characteristics you demonstrate that limit your wisdom. Look to your own beliefs and behaviors.

Add to the following list based on what you perceive:

<u>De-volved Self</u>		<u>Evolved Self</u>
Guarded	or	Vulnerable
Cover-up	or	Truth-telling
Masked	or	Authentic

3. Now to move on to action and commitment to be wise. Which of your evolving attributes or characteristics do you actively demonstrate through your work? List the wisdom-generating characteristics and the behaviors you currently or will start to demonstrate.

<u>Characteristic</u>	<u>Behavior</u>
Authentic	I learn from my work and act accordingly
Honest	I do what I say I will
Transparency	I am open about my business with everyone I work with

D. DEFINING & DEVELOPING WISDOM

Often what stops us from demonstrating wisdom is our lack of understanding as to what it is. Wisdom is not easily defined and therefore often unrecognizable when it surfaces. What is wisdom? How do we know when we are wise? Can wisdom be cultivated, or is it an innate gift? Our questioning alone causes confusion.

In an attempt to explore the concept of wisdom from a larger perspective, I've asked a number of my colleagues and clients for their input. I posed the following five questions. The responses, you will find, are heartwarming, insightful and, of course, wise. Please read over these as you contemplate your own answers.

1. How do you define wisdom?

✦ *Consideration of the whole. One can consider an issue contextually, holistically, systematically, strategically and morally. One may not have all the knowledge to study an issue, but a wise person will collaborate and take advantage of connected knowing to achieve wisdom. True wisdom embodies personal experience, yet transcends people and time.*

✦ *Individuals have wisdom because of the job they do and the insights that come to them as a result. Organizations also have wisdom, which they rarely tap (partly because they don't know how to). It takes place when individuals share their perspective which, of course, is their individual truth. In the process, everyone becomes smarter.*

✦ *I had hoped to come up with a clever answer. Alas, I came up with as many questions as statements. Neither knowledge nor intellect is wisdom. There seems to be an aching for wisdom—a way to give meaning to all the science and technology we rely upon in our day-to-day lives. Many of us know people who have great intellect and cognitive skills, but little wisdom; people who have little formal education and sophistication yet possess great wisdom; and people with both knowledge and wisdom.*

2. How do you know when you're acting from wisdom?

✦ *When you have a thorough understanding of an issue or situation, you can clearly see the impact of action or inaction. There is an emotional component of feeling clear with what may be a complex issue and a potentially gut-wrenching, unpopular decision. Furthermore, one feels confident from being open-minded and engaging in creative problem solving and seeking spiritual guidance.*

✦ *Wisdom provides perspective beyond the moment. I felt wise to advise my son to turn down a scholarship to pursue an education more in line with his dreams. We agreed the decision was about more than money. I felt the same in pursuing a business that failed and still do. My goal was to develop myself, and this provided the best path. The safer choice would be to repeat past experiences and may have actually concealed other risks.*

✦ *Wisdom seems to manifest when we least expect it. When we have great need of it and if we are fortunate, we take time to notice. We are surrounded by wisdom. Perhaps that's part of wisdom: noticing what's unnoticed by others.*

3. How can you cultivate a greater sense of wisdom?

✦ *By seeking understanding: first, of ourselves, in knowing how we construct our realities, our world; being clear about our emotional attachments to the issue and/or outcome; cultivating relationships with others we trust for their perspectives and complementary strengths; and by staying open to input from unexpected sources.*

✦ *First and foremost, slowing down to surrender to a force much larger and wiser than ourselves. Letting go of expectations and letting what is meant to happen take its course. Never being too good to do the mundane and be of service. Purposely putting yourself in areas of greater need. Keeping your ego in check—staying humble.*

✦ *Wisdom is about drawing on harmony, compassion and regard for our fellow travelers on this Earth. The wisdom of knowing that being right isn't necessarily the same as doing what's right. Wisdom is noticing, looking at possibilities by stepping outside our small self and joining with the larger Self. Wisdom is having compassion for those with whom we disagree. The greatest wisdom is loving-kindness for others in the face of unspeakable horror by realizing we are all part of the greater whole.*

4. What practices and disciplines have supported you in developing a greater sense of wisdom?

+ *Developing my intuitive knowing, my emotional knowing and my intellectual capabilities. I consider myself a lifelong learner. I collaborate with others to gain knowledge and bring a connected knowing to problems and work. I use creative problem solving. I open myself to information from less traditional sources such as my unconscious, the universe and spiritual guidance.*

+ *Being myself vs. what I thought someone else wanted me to be (maturity); being connected to people and experiencing them (social); being curious about people (questioning); realizing just how different we are, but how similar (needs and desires); trying to keep my mouth shut vs. my desire to be the center of attention (self-control).*

+ *Reading: spiritual books like the Serendipity Bible (with questions to consider) and Celebration of Discipline; award-winning books like Guns, Germs & Steel; business books that espouse principles, like Seven Habits, books on trends, creativity, leadership, communication, philosophy. Attending noteworthy plays and dramas that show how human life plays out and what people value and commit to. Completed a 2-year program of spiritual growth and relationship building. Fitness and Yoga. Fasting, meditation and prayer.*

5. In what ways can we use our wisdom to address the complex business problems we face today?

✦ *First by bringing our whole enlightened self to the work. To be tolerant of others' diverse ways of communicating and thinking; to be compassionate; listen; brainstorm and use our creativity; teach others and allow ourselves to learn; work for the greater whole and not our own individual rewards and outcomes. Ultimately, work as our highest self toward collective purpose.*

✦ *In business it is all about the people. The chiefs need the Indians and vice versa. No one is an island. Share your knowledge and experience with those behind and beside you. You reap what you sow (don't ever doubt that). Your success is dependent on others and vice versa. Life is more than work. Time is more than money — it's life itself. We are accountable to one another but to no one more than ourselves and our God. I can't help anyone else unless I help myself first (I can't share or teach what I don't have). Business and bureaucracy are beings in and of themselves and take on personalities — treat them as such.*

✦ *Break down the situation until actions we can take now become apparent. World Hunger ➤ a troubled country ➤ my country ➤ an organization ➤ donate money ➤ meet and help one person ➤ call United Way ➤ visit a food bank ➤ cook a dinner. Market share falling ➤ take a survey ➤ study product features ➤ call one customer who left us and ask them about it.*

✦ *Business decisions made from a greater whole, considering customers, stockholders, employees and greater humanity, are wise indeed. When businesses focus on issues of sustainability, their contribution to the community, as well as the value-added and triple bottom line, then they are demonstrating wisdom.*

At the next office meeting, start to ask yourself some questions that evolve wisdom:

1. Is our office culture supportive of all employees? Do we seek out and tap their wisdom and insights? If not, why not?
2. How can we be more of a world citizen, acting locally and thinking globally? Who can we help in our backyard?
3. Is our product, service or business philosophy causing any harm, regardless of how small? If so, what can we do about it?
4. Do we have a mission statement that is shared with everyone? Are we modeling our mission statement? If not, how do we start?

As I pondered the definition of Wisdom, I came across the following poem by R. D. Laing in a book by Julio Olalla, entitled *From Knowledge to Wisdom:*

> *"The range of what we think and do*
> *is limited by what we fail to notice.*
> *And because we fail to notice*
> *that we fail to notice*
> *there is little we can do*
> *to change*
> *until we notice*
> *how failing to notice*
> *shapes our thoughts and deeds."*

D. DEFINING & DEVELOPING WISDOM – HERE'S THE <u>CHALLENGE</u>.

Now it's your turn. Please answer the following questions—put them in your journal. I've added one additional question, beyond the ones on the previous pages, that I believe is the most important.

Thanks,
Patricia

1. How do you define wisdom?

2. How do you know when you're acting from wisdom?

3. How can you cultivate a greater sense of wisdom?

4. What practices and disciplines have supported you in developing a greater sense of wisdom?

5. In what ways can we use our wisdom to address the complex business problems we face today?

6. Given what you've just written, what small but important action(s) are you willing to take to develop and demonstrate YOUR wisdom at your work/business?

E. THE WISDOM-CENTERED VISIONARY™

Creating work from an enlightened frame of reference and new state of being requires the use of wisdom, which has been much of our focus in Tool 5. Hopefully, it is now a familiar companion. It will come to good use as we move forward. Wisdom is one of many powerful tools needed to create purposeful work that is viable in the marketplace. Vision is another. Together they are a force to be reckoned with.

Joining me in the unfolding of this Tool is Michelle James, CEO (Chief Emergence Officer) of The Center for Creative Emergence*. As I started to develop the outline, Michelle and her life's work came to mind. She is an extremely talented individual who focuses on the calling forth and emergence of the "new" through a creative process.

Here's why I'm involving her. The process of writing this book has been evolutionary for me—hopefully for you as well. I'm now beyond talking about working with others—I *am* working with others. As you know, this type of change is one of integration. What was a desire, then a need, is now a reality. This only happens as I move beyond some of my own barriers and fears. I'm pleased that this part of my evolution is finally in progress.

When Michelle and I first sat down we started with a clean slate. Honing in on the title and focus for this section was a process of emergence itself. We knew our task was to talk about tapping your creative and visionary nature, but we had not clearly defined the starting point, nor did we define the final destination. Through an iterative process, numerous insights surfaced. With a willingness to not know, we began to engage discovery. Through our dynamic interaction, a new level of clarity revealed itself. What emerged was the knowing that in order to advance to the next level of our evolution we must become Wisdom-Centered Visionaries.™

In these times it's not enough to be a creative visionary, for this can create good or evil. When we add wisdom to the mix, the essence of creation changes. It is steeped in the deeper self in a place of greater knowing and greater good. Results are more global, heartfelt and, of course, wise. There is a huge responsibility to a Wisdom-Centered Visionary™ that must be honored always. For we are the keepers of our visions and potentially the actualizers of a new world view.

A wisdom-centered vision is aligned with a higher purpose that extends above and beyond oneself. It is more than you—it works through you. It means opening up the mind, heart and soul to all that is possible. It's a new all-encompassing frame of reference from which we live our lives and do our work. It's always having the better good in mind as we do the hard work first. It holds up, embraces and supports a view of life and work that is soulful and generative.

Being a Wisdom-Centered Visionary™ is not always pretty, and certainly not easy or conventional. The path contains light and shadow, strength and vulnerability. It requires a different state of consciousness and a commitment to the highest good regardless of how rough the terrain.

Doing this work together is beyond anything we have done to date. As you know by now, we are always "being made ready," and this is undoubtedly the case here. If you have come this far, you are a courageous soul indeed—do not stop now. Playing small is a way of the past.

Living and working in the frame of a Wisdom-Centered Visionary™ is a way of life that demands a consciously conscious way of operating in the world. It's part of your evolutionary path.

Becoming a Wisdom-Centered Visionary™ is an over-time process. We've generated the following process to assist you in this development. These are emerging patterns we have observed and experienced in ourselves and others. You may know others—wisdom is expressed differently for each of us. You do know wisdom when you see it.

Start by reviewing the process on the next page with an open heart and mind. See which of the Frames, Actions and Results speak to you.

At this point you may feel enlivened, overwhelmed, awestruck,

Wisdom-Centered Visionary™ Process

Wisdom-Centered Visionary™ Frame of Reference	Action Needed to Call This Forth	Potential Results
Willingness to not know	Exploring the unknown	New outcomes beyond current frame of reference
Wholistic decision-making	Thinking outside of current patterns	Answers/solutions that have larger impact
Challenging assumptions	Questioning reality	Ability to create new realities
Taking risks never imagined	Intentionally setting higher risks	New growth & more influence
Living & working from a desired reality	Making action-based decisions from within	Desired circumstances benefit you & the larger system
Acknowledging a higher consciousness	Intentionally creating time to connect with it	Able to generate new options & choices
Knowing everything has a purpose	Extracting meaning	Learning from everything
A shadow side exists in all of us & every situation	Embracing the light & shadow	Feeling connected to your humanness & humanity
Knowing there is divinity in people & situations	Consciously practicing recognition	Your relationships are richer & generative
Living & working beyond the linear	Working with an expansive process	Making quantum leaps
Living & working from the future	Acting in the present based on a future vision	The future is now
Operating from the good of the whole	Always having the better good in mind in all decision-making	Exponential wins
Trailblazing	Operate from a new paradigm of thought	New system of thought becomes the accepted operating principle

hopeful—and any or all of these. We acknowledge that this internal shift may be easier said than done. For support and direction, we have come up with ways to allow this process to be more engaging. On the following pages are practices for getting started. Choose what fits and leave the rest.

Once you start expressing yourself as a Wisdom-Centered Visionary,™ as with any new awareness, it becomes easier. The ultimate goal is to integrate these new frames and actions into your life and work so they become the dominant mental model. The key is consistent engagement in your evolutionary development.

*Michelle James can be reached at:
The Center for Creative Emergence
www.creativeemergence.com
michelle@creativeemergence.com

E. THE WISDOM-CENTERED VISIONARY™ – HERE'S THE CHALLENGE:

Read over the following practices and choose what calls you. Do as many of these as you please.

Have fun with the exploration,
Patricia and Michelle

New Ways of Being:

1. Be willing to be a student of wisdom, life and purpose.
2. Expect wisdom to surface within yourself and, at the same time, help others call their wisdom forth.
3. Surround yourself with other wise individuals.
4. Allow yourself to have fun. Wisdom is to enjoy.

New Ways of Acting:

1. Make a wisdom collage. Get a big piece of paper and glue on pictures, draw images, write words, etc. Be sure these images express what wisdom is for you. Not just ancient wisdom, but present-day wisdom. Go beyond the conventional view. Don't let confusion stop you—get started, and inspiration will be your guide.

2. Identify and enact different ways of expressing your wisdom. This might look like dialoguing, journaling, drawing, movement, as well as other creative processes.

3. Create your own deck of wisdom cards. On 10 or so blank cards, write and draw images that express what wisdom is for you. When

done, reflect on these daily by picking a card and asking what it's telling you.

4. Explore what's preventing you from accessing your wisdom.
    a. Make a list of what you believe the blocks are to accessing your wisdom.
    b. Write down or draw what you believe is on the other side of these blocks.
    c. Draw or write about the pathway that takes you from where you are now to the other side— where your wisdom resides.

5. Design your own wisdom map. First step back and envision your path to wisdom. Allow your imagination to guide you—this is an invitation to explore new territory. What do you see and sense as you move down the path? What are the characteristics of the terrain? Let yourself be surprised!

TOOL 6

A CRITICAL TIME FOR WORK/BUSINESS EVOLUTION

A. *Work as an Expression of Love*

B. *Decision Making from Middle-Ground*

C. *Transforming Your Mental Frame of Reference*

D. *Evolving into the "Frame" of Purposeful Work*

A. Work as an Expression of Love

Tools 1 through 5 have been preparing us for this next step—sourcing our purpose from a renewed mental model of work. However, before we go any further, there is one last check we need to run on ourselves. We need to check the degree to which we are truly ready to create work realities that encourage both individual and business evolution—all toward self-actualization and transcendence.

We find ourselves at a critical time when the status quo is compromising our future. The wake-up calls are getting louder and stronger. Nothing less than a quantum leap will save us—from ourselves, that is. We need to know, without a doubt, that our work is meant to:

✦ *Evolve us as human beings*

✦ *Be a forum to share our gifts and talents for the greater good*

✦ *Heal inner wounds*

✦ *Be a platform for our calling and the callings of those we work with*

✦ *Evolve the model from which we work*

✦ *Be a viable, thriving entity in the marketplace*

✦ *Be an expression of love*

> *At a recent church service I attended, the minister talked about how we as human beings need to be a greater statement of love. What struck me was when she said that this was hard to do. As I see it, being a statement of love should be easy. What came next really rang true—to be a statement of love you have to let go of your righteousness, self-importance and ego. She reminded us that ego was Edging God Out!*

If we can get out of our own way, Purposeful work can be a statement of love. Here again was an example of how the old definition of work is all backwards. Being a statement of love through our work is one way in which we have a chance at righting the wrongs in the world today.

Are you ready for your work to be a statement of love? If so, are you prepared to let go of your righteousness and self-importance? Easier said than done—trust me.

We are in this together, so we might as well start now. Righteousness and self-importance show themselves in many ways. They rear their ugly heads when we:

✦ *Make others wrong in order to be right*

✦ *Play the game called my way or the highway*

✦ *Create separation instead of unity*

✦ *Put our needs ahead of the needs of others*

✦ *Do purposeful work as a part of ego gratification, not as a part of contribution and service*

This doesn't mean we aren't important and that we don't have rights. On the contrary, we *are* important, but not at the expense of anyone else. We have rights, preferences and desires, and they need to be expressed.

Nevertheless, we need to check our ego at the door, create humility and be thankful for the gift of purpose. Being a statement of love through our work is a tall order. As we take this on, we will be tested and given the opportunity to prove our commitment in some very humbling ways. We will also be blessed beyond our imagining, for this stand will feed and serve us.

Nothing can stop us from bringing our purpose to the marketplace with a stand as powerful as love. People will line up at our place of business, for love is so sorely missing and needed in the workplace and world today. Isolation and loneliness are rampant. People long for community, and today's work environment is working against everything we most need from a human perspective.

One of the techniques I use in my work is called falling in love with my client's potential. It focuses on embracing the individual's higher potential. Why not add this technique to your list as you practice being a statement of love.

As you progress through this Tool and envision your work purpose as a statement of love, remember that this vision is for you and those you serve. It is a motivator to keep you energized and a magnet to attract others. You are selling the love you have for the vision held so dearly—the vision of what is possible through your work. My hope is that you pass with flying colors.

"Work is love made visible."
– Kahlil Gibran

A. Work as an Expression of Love – Here's the Challenge:

The following exercises are meant to stretch you. Dig deep and go to a new place where your work is a statement of love. As always, take quiet time for answering the following.

Thank you so much,
Patricia

1. As you envision your new work future, where and how might self-righteousness and self-importance get in the way? Where might your ego be taking center stage? Not simple questions to ask or answer.

2. How is your work a statement of love? Give plenty of detail.

3. Is there a level of self-healing that might be needed at this time for your work to be a greater statement of love? If so, what might that be, and what is the benefit of taking this step now?

B. Decision Making from Middle-Ground

"It is my firm belief that in order to solve human problems in all their dimensions, we must combine and harmonize economic development with spiritual growth."
— His Holiness the Dalai Lama

Now I'm going to contradict myself. I've said our intellect is passé and that trusting our wisdom is the only way out of this mess we have gotten ourselves into. But if work is to be the incubator of the human spirit, we need to live it out as a human experience.

We live on this planet for a purpose. The manifestation of our purpose will happen with one foot firmly planted on earth and the other firmly planted in spirit. This new land of middle-ground will grant us the success we long for. Balancing the needs of working from purpose and making a living is the skill now needed. Creating our work purpose from what seems like nothing, packaging it to meet a need in the marketplace, developing the market and then selling it is a tall order (more on this in Tool 7). We need all the support we can get—from heaven and earth.

When we operate from the plane of existence, between heaven and earth, we can access the best of both worlds. It reminds me of the saying "We need to live in the world but not be part of it." Another similar saying is "We need to work *on* the business not *in* the business." In essence, we need to operate from a point of greatest perspective— detached but fully present.

This place is different for everyone. Only you know the balance where life and work is not a struggle but a blessing for you. It is not the extremes of the highs and lows, the far left and right, nor solely the light in lieu of the dark that will create new work realities. The pendulum of life needs to swing to the center, firmly rooted in middle-ground, primed to develop purpose.

If middle-ground is not familiar territory, you may sense an internal tug of resistance. You may be feeling one of many things. If you are used to living in the extremes, middle-ground may seem like a compromise, a giving up of an ideal, or giving in to a way of life that goes against the grain. You may have established comfort living and working in the extremes—the ethers or security at all cost. Neither will get you what you want or what the world needs. If this is your master, you have bought into a false god.

> *I realized a while back that I was neglecting my financial well-being and living in the extreme that spirit will take care of me. I'm not saying that spirit doesn't take care, but I do need to do my part. This thing called codependence can exist with any entity, not just other humans.*

> *I am reminded, yet again, that I haven't fully learned this lesson. I am in midyear and find myself looking at low financial projections. This year started out better than the last few, but an old pattern has surfaced again. I have more faith in the future than I have in the present. This causes neglect on my part of the day-to-day realities of life and work. This is the extreme I tend to live in. I forget that the present seeds the future.*

It's time to engage a new middle-ground that will mainstream our work so feeding our pocketbooks and soul becomes commonplace. The miracles of our purpose will start to appear as we come to center, grounded in passion, purpose and new productivity. What appeared stuck will loosen. What was always there will surface to embrace and bring forth.

Having the gift to access the power of heaven and earth should not be taken lightly. Its presence will be there as long as it is honored.

I'd like to end this section with something very dear to me. It is a prayer I found in my father's workshop and at the same time, my mother's bedroom. Who would have guessed!

Native American Prayer

"O great Spirit, whose voice I hear in the winds, and whose breath gives life to all the world, hear me! I am small and weak; I need your strength and wisdom. Let me walk in beauty and make my eyes ever behold the red and purple sunset. Make my hands respect the things you have made and my ears sharp to hear your voice. Make me wise so that I may understand the things you have taught my people. Let me learn the lessons you have hidden in every leaf and rock. I seek strength, not to be greater than my friend, but to fight my greatest enemy—myself. Make me always ready to come to you with clean hands and straight eyes. So when life fades, as the fading sunset, may my spirit come to you without shame."

– Red Cloud Indian School, Pine Ridge, SD
(Used by permission.)

B. Decision Making from Middle-Ground – Here's the Challenge:

Please take the quiet time necessary to do the following exercises.

Thank you,
Patricia

1. Take a few deep breaths, close your eyes and bring yourself into the present moment. With feet flat on the ground and a sense of spirit at your side, get a sense of your center, your middle-ground. Stay here for 5–10 minutes and let whatever wants to surface appear.

2. Now write about what you sensed, saw or felt. What does your middle-ground feel and look like? Do you sense any internal resistance? Write down whatever comes up.

3. On a day-to-day basis, what is middle-ground for you? How do you need to be living your life and work to stay centered in heaven and earth? What might be off-center?

C. Transforming Your Mental Frame of Reference

In working through the Seven Evolutionary Tools, we have been preparing ourselves for this next shift. Hopefully, we are now ready for an internal transformation that could shake our world. It's an unfamiliar place for many because it is exactly that—the unfamiliar. A frame of reference of life and work that hasn't existed up to now, that hasn't been made available because, honestly, we weren't ready.

If we are ready and willing to do the work, then our life will never be the same. We will have evolved into a new energetic field, frame of reference and mental model of how we operate in the world.

We have made great progress. It is now time for more; it's time for transformation. We are not going from A to B this time. This quantum leap is an A to M, N, O and P. It's an 180° change in the scheme of things.

We have no choice—if we are to save ourselves and our planet. The clock is ticking in terms of global warming, the depletion of the ozone layer, the next pandemic. The rising obesity rate and general fear are sedating individuals into non-action when what's needed is radical action.

This next "right" action is often made clear when I see it playing itself out in myself and my clients. I've learned to pay attention when a pattern keeps recurring. At present, what is surfacing is twofold. The first I call *Letting go of the past limited image of self.* The second is *Stepping into and testing out a new persona.* The last remains of old patterning is being stripped away. It goes far beyond the current beliefs we hold. It is broader, deeper and more entrenched. It is generational in nature and is the ultimate hard wiring.

Moving into radical action and the next level of our work future requires us to develop new internal reference points to validate this new world view. If we have nothing to match it up against in our current reality, it doesn't exist. It doesn't register as a possibility. It goes in one ear and out the other. We don't see it, hear it or sense it and thus don't act on it. We are blind to the possibility and the opportunity.

I now believe that we can't embrace this new world of work if we can't internally reference it. We can't be and act from this new frame if we aren't able to comprehend or validate its possibility.

The frame of reference we hold is our check-and-balance system. It has been developed, refined and reinforced over years of life experience. It provides the definition of our known world. We believe it enables a sense of safety and security—but does it? In truth, it may be providing a comfort level that often holds us back.

As your reference points start to expand, your comfort level will be challenged, along with your very identity. Physical and mental sensations may occur as you change from the inside out. Know that this is all good—great, actually.

> These internal shifts can be disconcerting. The first time I felt a physical reaction to this frame of reference shift was around 1987. It felt like my DNA was being rewritten. My whole body was vibrating—for days. It was scary. A healer I was seeing at the time told me to focus on the routine in my life, like eating and sleeping, to create stability.
>
> I've felt this physical realignment many times since. Mentally it's like the synapses in my brain were reconfiguring themselves. I could actually feel movement in my head. The vibrational level of my very existence was quickening.
>
> Once this starts you have little to say in the matter. This isn't something to try to understand at an intellectual level. You won't find an answer. When this happens now, I'm mostly excited and thankful because I know it is evolution at work.

As the larger frame of reference and image of ourselves and what is possible through our work transforms, we create from a larger whole. We start to think from the future. We are now able to envision a powerful future because we can affirm its existence within ourselves. Our new internal reference points validate this.

The world can now present us with opportunities we couldn't see before. They are handed to us. They appear in our mind's eye and then actualize as we watch. This is a powerful place to be, so be grateful for its presence. We are at a point in our evolution when new work futures can manifest more quickly and more easily than ever before.

Don't be surprised if you fight yourself on this one. Our old frame is very entrenched, and the ego isn't going to let go without some kicking and screaming. Your comfort zone and old "small" self will be seriously put to a test.

EVOLUTIONARY WORK CASE STUDY

BEV HITCHINS

Purposeful Business Circle Member

Changing my frame of reference has been my biggest challenge as I create my business, ALIGN, A Unique and Integrative Approach to Clutter and Balance. I have had to let go of my smaller self—the one that screeches, "What makes you an expert? Who do you think you are? Who are you fooling?" In fact, ever since I launched ALIGN, I have had to chisel away at that traditional mindset Patricia describes in this Tool. My work is about opening space in my clients' lives so that their true selves can emerge and flourish—or maybe it's about creating space in my own life for my true self to emerge and flourish.

At the same time my smaller self was screeching, my larger true self was working undercover. By my taking small steps followed by larger ones, my true self began to counter those questions with "Just wait a minute! I've got something valuable to offer! I am going to ignore you and push ahead." Oh, there have been minefields along the way—most of them self-sabotaging ploys to keep me back at the starting gate—but each time that happens I learn something new about myself, gain another thimbleful of confidence and get moving. I just can't go back to where I was!

Do know that your new work future has the universe on its side. It won't allow you to continue to play small. Your choice points are shifting and expanding, and there is no turning back. You are once again at the point of no return.

It's now your time and turn to access a new frame from which to do your work. And we are with you every inch of the way, for this step is almost impossible to do alone. Also, know and gain comfort in the fact that, in some way, you have experienced this before and it's time for the next level.

C. Transforming Your Mental Frame of Reference – Here's the Challenge:

Take the following pre-steps to align yourself for change. Let it come and you'll be in for an exciting road ahead. If you are after true change, then the following Challenge can't be bypassed.

It is time,
Patricia

1. First and foremost: surrender. Let any resistance just fall. Release it immediately. Know that the universe has your better good in mind, so let it now lead. Follow the guidance, clues, patterns and wisdom within you. Listen to what all parts of you are whispering in your ear. Write about what happens or might happen when you truly do this.

2. Take extra care of yourself as the internal/external shift occurs. Be open to a new level of healing work. What would it look like if you took better care of yourself? This is a long list and one to start acting on now.

3. Create even more quiet introspective time. Morning, noon and night—fill your life with quiet. You can do this. Write about how this will occur and what the benefit will be.

4. It's time to let out the creative spiritual flow within you. You may now find yourself waking up earlier in the mornings. If so, take heed of the Rumi quote: "The morning breeze has secrets to tell you—do not go back to sleep." What might this look like?

D. Evolving into the "Frame" of Purposeful Work

"The future belongs to a very different kind of person with a very different kind of mind—creators and expathizers, pattern recognizers and meaning makers. These people— artists, inventors, designers, storytellers, caregivers, consolers, big picture thinkers—will now reap society's richest rewards and share its greatest joys."

— "Whole New Mind: Why Right-Brainers Will Rule the Future," Daniel H. Pink

Evolution is BANGING at our door. The polite knock is a thing of the past. It's now louder, clearer, and the questions just won't leave us alone:

✦ *Are you ready, willing and able to shift the present-day limiting reference points to create a renewed future?*

✦ *Will you give the time and conjure the fortitude knowing a quick fix is not the answer?*

✦ *Can you hold out, in spite of the fear that certainly will surface, for the sake of the greater good?*

Evolving into the "frame" of purposeful work is about maturing into our rightful place. We who work from spirit and wisdom have the skills to heal the marketplace.

The outdated limiting energies are ready to be transmuted—if we first do our part. When released from generational patterns of "not enough," codependency, self-destruction, self-pity and self-sabotage, a higher vibrational pattern can then take over.

A higher degree of emotional maturity and spiritual growth is now called for. If we are to model and develop a new enlightened work world, then it's time to enlist the new frame of purposeful work and evolve.

I must share this with you because it's quite a startling revelation. All of a sudden, it feels like my past dysfunctional frame of reference had just dissipated and a new frame has been created. It feels like a switch was clicked and that I'm now operating from a new and different set of reference points—previously inaccessible. The old frame is literally going, going, gone—as if it never existed.

I now have at my fingertips a stronger frame of reference that is expansive, positive, proactive, enlivening, enlightening and fun! This is amazing unto itself. I look forward to fully playing in this exponential expansion from the inside out and feeling its power and strength.

D. Evolving into the "Frame" of Purposeful Work – Here's the Challenge:

The following Challenge is meant to physically, mentally and emotionally assist in evolving us beyond the next layer of "holding" still present. At some level we have done this before, but it's now time to dig deeper. Once done, our essence will have a greater chance to expand, letting evolution take over.

Let's get started. You will need: soft meditative music to soothe the soul, candles to light the way and a blanket to comfort the body.

We are in this together,
Patricia

Step One – Releasing at a Physical Level

1. Stand so you have an arm's length all around you.
2. Take a couple of very deep breaths.
3. You want to loosen up the hold that the past has on you by first loosening up the body. Start moving as if you are shaking loose the past. Shake it off, wiggle it away, let it flow out of you. Keep taking deep breaths as you do this.
4. Shake off the past as you focus on releasing 1) Any physical pain you may be holding that keeps you stagnant; 2) A false image of your body as anything less than perfect; or 3) Any dis-ease and its physical manifestation.
5. Listen to what your body is telling you in the form of aches and pains. These are reminders of lessons to be learned. Our bodies are meant to move with grace, to be healthy vehicles for our spirits, and to carry us into long, wonderful lives.
6. Keep shaking. Let it all go!

7. When you feel complete stop, take a couple of very deep breaths and release even further.
8. Repeat as necessary—even daily for awhile.

Step Two – Releasing at an Emotional Level

1. Lying comfortably on the floor, close your eyes and take a couple of long deep breaths. Put on some music and let it comfort you. Use a blanket, if necessary, to keep you warm.
2. Think of yourself being embraced by what you know as your higher power. The arms of unconditional love envelop you. This love is all around you. It sparkles, shines and is blissful. You feel supported like never before.
3. Now welcome any limiting emotions or feelings to surface. They could be loneliness, anger, guilt, shame, a feeling of not enough— you name yours. They may be limitations from the past, passed down from mother or father, grandparents, great-grandparents, that you no longer want to continue and that weren't rightfully yours in the first place.
4. You are in a safe place, so let yourself feel these feelings. Let them surface and flow through you. Don't resist.
5. Release anything that is inhibiting your evolution and ultimately the evolution of those you work with, anything that is preventing happiness and joy, or anything that is getting in the way of your living out the life and work that you are meant to.
6. When you feel complete, take a couple of very deep breaths and let go at an even deeper level.

Step Three – Expanding into Your Essence

1. Stand up and take a few deep breaths.
2. As you breathe, begin to expand your energy out from your body in all directions. Going up from your head, down from your feet,

out from your sides and all around you. Stretch your arms out and move them around. You can sense the field of your being expanding further than it ever has. Your reach has doubled—even quadrupled.

3. Maintaining this expansive stance requires practice. So first thing each morning practice expanding and holding this field for as long as possible. If you lose your connection, just do numbers 1 and 2 again.

4. Give this expansive stance a symbol or name and then conjure this up to assist in all your work and business affairs.

5. Now, when inspired, your new mental frame of reference will start to surface. It will consist of new thoughts, beliefs, feelings and actions. Write about and/or draw what is now becoming so apparent as a new way of life and work expression. Be as specific as you can. Use the image below as a container for what you write/draw.

6. Begin to talk with others about what it looks like to live and work from this new frame. Tell as many people as possible—except the naysayers. Spread the word.

TOOL 7

PURPOSEFUL WORK – THRIVING IN THE MARKETPLACE

A. *Solidifying Your Purpose, Vision & Mission*

B. *Meeting Deeper Needs in the Marketplace*

C. *Building Relationships – Attracting the Right Audience*

D. *Strategically Creating from the Future*

A. Solidifying Your Purpose, Vision and Mission

Using the last six Tools you have worked very diligently to create a solid internal foundation that will now act to firmly support your new work structure. So, roll up your sleeves because it's time to create the external foundation for your work or business of choice. We'll start with developing a purpose, vision, mission statement all the way up to strategically planning your work/business for the future. This will require that fine line of "being in the flow" and also doing your part.

The way this Tool is formatted is again a reflection of my own evolution as I've written this book. It's as much my words as it is the words of those I've worked with. It's their work world that needs sharing and from which we have much to learn. You will find their examples inspirational. They will lend guidance and support as you write your own.

(As a way to highlight and recognize these individuals, you will find more information on their work and businesses at the back of the book.)

A-1. YOUR PURPOSE STATEMENT – THE TIP OF THE UMBRELLA

The purpose statement is where we will start. It is the point from which everything else evolves. It's like the tip of an umbrella, with the spokes as your services and/or products.

Your purpose statement is the following and so much more; it:

✦ *Is more holistic, evolutionary and transformational in nature than vision or mission.*

✦ *It resonates and aligns with your essence. You are it and it is you.*

✦ *Is a longing in your life and the future you want in the world.*

✦ *Calls and leads you daily to expand, like a magnet drawn to a greater outcome.*

✦ *It is evolutionary in nature—evolving you and those impacted.*

✦ *Is fulfilled in the present and at the same time "readies" you for the future.*

✦ *Inspires commitment, innovation and courage.*

✦ *Transforms a dream into a reality.*

✦ *Is meant to be, and at some level you know this.*

✦ *Addresses the often-perplexing question of "Why am I here?"*

Just speaking your purpose statement begins to shift the energetic field and the viewpoint from which you live and work. Writing it and acting on it can change the world.

The format of this statement is present tense. It is action oriented. There is a *from* piece and a *to* piece. It states a desired result. It may, at first, seem vague and general, and that's OK; details can be added later in the vision and mission statements.

The following are examples to read, reflect on and use as guidance.

Dave of iWavz, LLC
states his purpose as:

Empathetically connecting people with innovative ideas that can solve problems and improve today's hope and tomorrow's fulfillment by exploring the known and conceiving what may come next.

Christine states her purpose in a poem called "The Poet":

I am an ocean,
hauling treasures from the depths,
heaving them on shore
with tranquil
or tempestuous throes.
A wanderer,
lonely with longing,
stoops to lift a seashell from the
sand, admires its honed,
exquisite beauty
and holding it against an ear,
hears, at last, clear voices of the
ageless deep echoing
the vast, unspeakable soul.

Karen, of JLII Associates, says the following:

Our overarching purpose is to create environments and experiences which inspire, educate and support individuals to perform with heightened competencies and leadership.

Pam, in developing
her purpose, says:

My purpose is to bring excitement, kindness and deep meaning to events and experiences for myself and others. This is done through movement, music, rhythm, spiritual depth and love.

Linda, from Peace Through Travel and Women's Peace Through Travel, is clear that her purpose is:

We contribute to the alleviation of the poverty and suffering of women and children by connecting women globally through business and travel.

A-1. Your Purpose Statement – The Tip of the Umbrella – Here's the <u>Challenge</u>:

It's now time to "draft" your purpose statement. Remember that there is no right or wrong. What you write now may change over time, and that's OK. Make this statement one that is larger than you and that you can grow into.

Thanks, this is important work,
Patricia

Use the following as a guideline for this challenge:

1. Close your eyes.
2. Take a couple very deep breaths.
3. Quiet your mind—ask your greater purpose to surface.
4. Feel the feelings that come up—this part is very important.
5. Let your mind, body and spirit expand outward. Stay in this space for 3–5 minutes or more as this statement is given birth.
6. As you are doing this, consider what was discussed in this section.
7. Use the space below to write down whatever surfaces. Write the statement about your purpose. Don't censor nor judge.

Have fun!

A-2. Your Vision Statement – The World You Want to See!

Your vision statement is a reflection of what you want to see in the world. It may be an aspect or need that appears to be "missing" and that you would like to create or enhance. It's a living picture of your dreams and desires turned into words. Let your purpose statement, from the last section, act as a guide for your vision.

There are a number of approaches you might take to developing and writing your vision statement. Following are a few ideas to test out:

+ *A fun approach is to answer this question: If a visitor from Mars dropped in, what would your visitor see and sense? Write your vision statement in the future tense.*

+ *Let your mind, body and spirit expand beyond itself three years into the future. Begin to bring up a vision of what is possible. Think of what year this will be. Hold this vision for 3–5 minutes or more as it comes into view*

+ *If visualizing isn't an easy task for you, start by focusing on how your future work/business might make you feel, then put these feelings into words and pictures.*

+ *See the benefits of your vision for others. What will happen as others are influenced by your vision?*

There are innumerable ways to develop a vision statement. Mine are fairly straight forward and easy. Just keep it simple and let it flow.

Here again are examples of vision statements, from individuals who have participated in this work. For the sake of this exercise we are using three years as our future vision point. I hope these both inform and inspire you to get started developing your own.

Karen states her vision as:

Our work is instrumental in creating and sustaining workplaces and communities of people worldwide who are performing at their highest capacity, being creatively productive, living abundantly and in harmony with one another.

How Pam sees her vision:

Masks are dropped, inhibitions released and we naturally and lovingly share in movement circles, singing, crying, laughing, playing and discovering who we really are together in community.

Linda's vision is:

We see women connecting across political, cultural and socioeconomic boundaries through business and travel for mutual learning, support and, ultimately, the betterment of our world.

The vision for International Purpose and myself, three years into the future, looks like:

Hundreds of individuals are working together in Purposeful Business Circles laughing, generating innovative enlightened business ideas, planning higher level risks, healing deep-seated patterns, supporting and keeping each other accountable. Our relationships with both businesses and individuals with similar missions have enabled us to expand exponentially. PBCs are now growing in many major cities and small villages worldwide. Our train-the-trainer sessions have drawn dozens of individuals. We are now seen as one of the upcoming businesses leading transformational work.

The spider plant image below is our representation of our business chart. The pot nurtures and blossoms the people and information at the core of our work.

A-2. Your Vision Statement – The World You Want to See! – Here's the Challenge:

This is the time to draft your vision statement. Remember that what you see or sense is yours to manifest. We are all unique, and this statement is a unique expression of your work in the world.

Have at hand lots of colored markers.

Have fun with this,
Patricia

Use the following as guidelines for this Challenge:

1. Close your eyes and put a smile on your face.
2. Take a few deep breaths.
3. Calm your mind—ask for your vision to surface.
4. Feel the feelings that arise.
5. Let your mind, body and spirit expand outward three years into the future. Begin to bring up a vision of what is possible. Think of what year this will be. Hold this vision for 3–5 minutes or more as it comes into view.
6. As you are doing this, consider the guidelines from this section.
7. Using the space below, draw and write what you see or sense—your vision statement. Anything goes!

RITA J. MIRISCIOTTI
Coaching Client

The year 2000 was highly anticipated by many but proved to be of 'millennial' proportions for me as it was the start of what would be a profound, life-changing experience. It was then that I met Patricia DiVecchio and the International Purpose model that would take me from my "stable and good" job (that was slowly suffocating me) to a world of no limits and being able to breathe again. I would go from being unhappy, unchallenged and working and living in an area that only depressed me to being motivated, exhilarated and aware of my role in the Big Picture of life.

Through one-on-one work with International Purpose, I began to expand my world of "I can" and "I will" through abstract homework that built a foundation for a plan. I began to explore my unique talents, skills and abilities and pursue my passion for wine, food and culture. Volunteering at a local winery in exchange for learning how to make wine led me to create my own position with the winery as a part-time marketing rep. I was at the point of no return and could no longer stay where I was. The Seven Evolutionary Tools had affected a profound change in who I was and resurrected me. I moved from my home, an hour from Pittsburgh, to a new home 20 minutes from the city, full of everything I loved and craved. Once again I created my own position, this time with my full-time employer and near my new home, where I finally fit in. This was the transitional step I needed to make the most risky, but most necessary, change in my life if I were to realize my goals, dreams and true purpose.

In January 2005 I retired/resigned from my position of 17 years at the university and developed a plan to realize my dream business and the concepts of Wine Consulting and the Edu-Social Wine Experience. By 2009 I opened my own wine tasting room and restaurant in Pittsburgh and am sharing this "edu-social" and "unique" wine experience with others. It has been a wonderfully exciting, sometimes scary but always rewarding and satisfying experience. I am still learning and evolving but realize how important this process was, is and will be. My newfound strength and faith in who I am and what I do assures me that I will be more than just fine...I will be great!

A-3. YOUR MISSION STATEMENT – THE MEANS TO YOUR PURPOSE

Your mission brings form to your purpose and vision. It is the means and way to manifest your work in the world. It dissects and bisects your purpose into actionable ways of being and acting. It takes your vision and defines the path to its creation.

It is the most concrete statement of the three. It works in tandem with your two previous statements. Your mission statement is the answer to these questions:

1. What will I be doing?
2. What will my business offer, and how will it be unique?
3. What are the results desired?
4. What difference does my work make in the world?
5. At what level does my work "heal" those that it serves?

Every noun, adjective and verb in your mission statement is important—as is true for all three statements. You will want this statement to express your work/business objectives in a way that inspires support and ongoing commitment.

Write it in the present tense using proactive verbs. Don't make it too lengthy—this is meant to be a broad perspective and short enough so that anyone connected to the work can readily repeat it.

As you write your mission statement, use your purpose and vision statements as a reference. Remember that everything starts from purpose and that your mission should be a reflection of your higher calling.

Two business examples are:

✦ *Planet 3000 is committed to healing the earth through advocacy, by researching natural ecosystems, developing policy recommendations and piloting demonstration projects that apply these underlying principles to human ecosystems that are in harmony with other life on the planet.*

✦ *Fast Company's mission states: "We believe that work isn't simply a paycheck; it is the ultimate expression of a fully realized self. We believe that a company's obligations extend far beyond its bottom line and its shareholders—to a wider constituency that includes employees, customers, suppliers and the community."*

Following are examples to reflect on and learn from:

DENICE, FOUNDER AND PRESIDENT OF MANAGANCE CONSULTING, STATES THE FOLLOWING AS THEIR MISSION:

We facilitate powerful strategic thinking processes that integrate consulting and coaching to move leaders of socially responsible organizations everywhere to deeper levels of investment in management. This investment results in higher levels of performance and fresh opportunities.

KAREN STATES HER MISSION AS:

JLH Associates is a catalyst that inspires open dialogue, stimulates learning and facilitates purposeful action which leads to individual and organizational excellence. We guide people through experiences which encourage the growth of leadership capacity and the sustainability of healthier organizations and communities.

CYNTHIA, OF THE HYGEIA WELL BEING CENTER AND THE UNIVERSITY OF VIRGINIA, STATES HER TWO MISSIONS AS:

The University of VA's Nutrition Counseling Center – We offer expert coaching in healthful eating, biobehavioral strategies and Medical Nutrition Therapy to adults and children who wish to improve their health. Our overall mission is to prevent, slow or reverse disease and enable measurable healthy well-being in our clients. The Hygeia Well Being Center – First, we provide transformational evidence-based healthy living education to adults and children. Second, we enable mental and physical health, human development, the experience of joy and reduction of suffering and disease.

LINDA STATES HER MISSION AS:

Our Global Action Network exists to join entrepreneurial women in the West with women in the developing world who are lifting themselves out of poverty through their own entrepreneurialism. Women Travel for Peace provides Western women the opportunity to work side-by-side with our sisters-in-need abroad for a mutually enriching and unforgettable experience.

A-3. YOUR MISSION STATEMENT –
THE MEANS TO YOUR PURPOSE –
HERE'S THE <u>CHALLENGE</u>:

This mission statement is your "call to action" for yourself, your work/business associates and those you serve. Write it so all are left inspired.

Job well done,
Patricia

Use the following as guidelines for this Challenge:

1. Close your eyes and relax.
2. Take a few deep breaths.
3. Calm your mind—ask for your mission to surface.
4. Feel the feelings that arise.
5. Consider the guidelines from this section.
6. Write what comes up for you that is most compelling. Write your mission statement.

A-4. Guiding Principles & Core Values

"Values rely on the spiritual dimension. If free markets
are to thrive, ordinary investors—like you and me—
must again trust business. That will not happen
until we believe the culture and philosophy of business
have transformed. And only people can create
a shift in corporate consciousness.
All the system knows is how to survive.
It does not know how to heal itself. But you and I do.
We know the only way to save the patient is
with an infusion of consciousness and values."
– "Megatrends 2010," Patricia Aburdene

This section explores the guiding principles and core values that you want to incorporate into your work/business. These are the backdrop to all action and decision-making. They are often very subtle but are very important.

Let's first take a look at guiding principles. A working definition might be "standards held as a way to direct yourself and your work." They govern the operation of your work and its relationship with society, customers, suppliers, employees, local community, other stakeholders and ultimately self.

Your guiding principles are statements of belief, of knowing, and they are foundational to the core of who you are and what your work/business is about. They are standards that guide your thinking and your actions.

Values are attributes that are a reflection of your essence and, in turn, your business's. These could be physical values, such as reliability or high quality; organizational, such as accountability or cooperation; or psychological in nature, as is harmony or service to society. Values are usually stated in one or two words.

Walt Disney, an entertainment business, states their values as follows:

> *"No cynicism*
> *Nurturing and promulgation of*
> *'wholesome American values'*
> *Creativity, dreams and imagination*
> *Fanatical attention to consistency and detail*
> *Preservation and control of the Disney 'magic.'"*

Canada's Embassy Graphics, based in Winnipeg, espouses the values of:

> *"Truth and love and styles itself as a 'modern day*
> *community' where business means more than pursuing*
> *profit and people can grow, develop—and make money."*

Our guiding principles and values are meant to be lived. We aspire daily to demonstrate these in our work and business. They are reminders of what we stand for. They are determined through careful self-examination of what is most important. They inform us about ourselves. The proof of their existence shows up in the congruence among self and work and the perception of others.

The only example that follows is my own. I hope you will be inspired and learn from the following.

Guiding Principles and Values
of International Purpose:

✦ We believe we are in the midst of a rapidly evolving time where both human and work systems are quickly transforming. International Purpose works to provide tools and support for this effort toward the creation of a highly functional, humanistic and humane work model.

✦ Everyone has a unique purpose that can act as a means to evolve and heal.

- ✦ Our goal is to influence as many people as possible as we meet both human and work needs and make a viable global impact.
- ✦ This work works through us—we are the instrument and conduit. We are energetically shifting the way we see and define ourselves, our purpose and the work world. We therefore need to always be doing the work to clarify ourselves. "We can't take a client to where we haven't first gone ourselves."
- ✦ Our belief is that viable and thriving work and business is possible for everyone with a clearly defined purpose and the courage to do the hard "inner" work necessary to bring it to reality.
- ✦ Life and work are to learn from—we are students and teachers at the same time.
- ✦ A global reach can only happen through relationships and in partnerships with many like-minded individuals.

Core Values

- ✦ Compassion
- ✦ Integrity
- ✦ Honesty
- ✦ Lifelong learning & reflection
- ✦ Respect & appreciation for self and others
- ✦ Self-responsibility
- ✦ Creation of community & unity
- ✦ Steward leadership
- ✦ Financial stewardship
- ✦ Self-care
- ✦ Inclusivity
- ✦ A belief in human nature

✦ Endless possibilities
✦ Optimism
✦ Transparency
✦ Faith & trust in a power greater than ourselves
✦ Love

A-4. GUIDING PRINCIPLES & CORE VALUES – HERE'S THE CHALLENGE:

The following are questions to contemplate as you determine the guiding principles and core values from which you and your work/business are to operate. These are part of your work foundation and a reflection of what you do daily.

Give the following good thought,
Patricia

I. Guiding Principles

1. What guides you and your work or business to do good in the world?
2. What higher standards do you hold for your work/business?

II. Values

1. What is most important in terms of how you interact with others?
2. How do you treat others?
3. What attributes do you model in your day-to-day work life?

Write what you currently know and then add to that list over time.

B. Meeting Deeper Needs
in the Marketplace

Now, with your greater purpose written, your vision firmly in your mind's eye and your mission in concrete terms, you can move onto the next step. Now is the time to identify how your work purpose can meet the deeper human and emotional needs in the marketplace.

Then and only then can others be "touched" by what you have to offer. Your job is to add structure to your work so it can be presented to the marketplace in a way others can value and purchase.

Your offering, once crafted into your service and/or product, will attract the right audience. When done, nothing will stop you from making the impact desired and in turn gaining a worthy reward.

"When I speak of the business of desire,
I am talking to every one of us. The politics of desire
is a basic dynamic of life. It includes any pursuit that
lives by the mysterious laws of has/gets: the marketplace
itself, management and diplomacy, politics and policy,
relationships and romance, religion and war,
power and fame. In all of the heart-and-mind
fields of life, those people with the keenest understanding
of how to address human desire ultimately prevail."

– "The New Culture of Desire:
5 Radical New Strategies That Will
Change Your Business and Your Life,"
Melinda Davis

B-1. Identifying the Deeper "Emotional" Needs in the Marketplace

Our greater purpose is calling us to address deeper human needs in the world today. These needs go beyond the material to bringing meaning and healing to our lives. They are often of an emotional or spiritual nature and address our very essence. These needs may or may not be at a conscious level. They sometimes sit in the place where we know that we don't know.

These basic human needs tend to surface as a longing for community, a desire for greater purpose, a need for security and/or a need for greater human and spiritual connection. They show up as longing for more joy, understanding or love. They may result in sorrow and sadness, physical pain, or lack of confidence.

At some level, we are all crying out, in silence or action, to have these needs met. The work of addressing these needs is the work of the times and of evolution itself. They differ based on the society and culture we live in, as well as on what is happening in our lives at any one time.

Here again I'd like to reference Maslow's Hierarchy of Needs. Our greater work purpose is about evolving to higher level needs and helping others do the same. For as our work impacts and heals us, it heals others. We then become the catalyst for greater meaning and evolution.

At the levels of self-actualization and transcendence we are able to "touch" a core in others so that transformation occurs. We then have the opportunity to end the human cycle of repeating the past and thereby create freedom to develop the future of choice. As you can see we all have very special work to do.

So what are the deeper human needs you are meant to address and heal through YOUR work? How do you begin to recognize them so you and your work can be of best service? As always, you start with yourself and those closest to you.

Knowing the deeper needs in the marketplace requires us to start close to home. Understanding our own needs and the needs of those closest to us will tell us much. Since we all hold the consciousness of the human race, the pain, longing and passion we each experience are universal in many ways. In the end we all want and long for the same basic things.

B-1. IDENTIFYING THE DEEPER "EMOTIONAL" NEEDS IN THE MARKETPLACE – HERE'S THE <u>CHALLENGE</u>:

Use the following questions to help surface the deeper needs your work is meant to address. As you know by now, the harder the question, the more insightful the answer. You may choose to answer all questions or a select few. The responses that keep repeating themselves are the ones to pay attention to. When doing this Challenge, conjure up your sense of greater wisdom that reflects all of humanity.

Give this time,
Patricia

1. Reflecting on Maslow´s Hierarchy of Needs, what basic human needs do you see as prevalent in your world at this time?

2. Same question in a different way: What is currently missing in life and at work/business?

3. From an emotional or spiritual level, what are others saying is most important to them at this time?

4. What needs, when met, will help people evolve to a higher level of potential?

5. If you could summarize your responses into two or three core needs, what would those be?

B-2. MATCHING YOUR WORK PURPOSE TO THE NEED(S) IN THE MARKETPLACE

Now that you have identified some of the core needs in the marketplace, it's time to do the matching to your work/business. This is an inside-out process that is true for all of our work together.

This section is brought to life through a question-and-answer format that illustrates how others have matched their purpose to deeper needs in the marketplace. These examples are from individuals like you, creating purposeful work as viable and thriving in the marketplace.

The responses are those of individuals I've worked with over the years, as well as my own. As you read these, do be thinking of your own replies. I hope you are left inspired to write your own.

Question #1: How did you realize that your unique skills could be used as part of "new" work or business in the marketplace?

A. Ryta answered with this:

Frankly, through the process of working with Patricia I realized I could take my skills and create work from them—not the reverse that is much more common. I began to realize that I didn't have to necessarily get another "job."

First I had to realize I had unique skills and then second that they could be used for new work. Over time, I realized that through my own unique skills of education and performance, my experiences within the wine industry and my ability to make people feel at ease, I could meet a need that was very present in the wine industry.

In addition, others began to tell me I should do this type of work once they realized I wanted to do my own business. They knew my skills and gave me suggestions.

B. While Dave answered this way:

I had already found my way into consulting and had developed a mission statement of "connecting people with concepts to improve life." Where I struggled was with narrowing to a sharper focus to produce a clear value proposition. Both my strength and my weakness is my broad base of knowledge and experiences. I believe my success is found in a series of focuses, from which generalized principles and an approach can be drawn. It doesn't matter what the business is because it's about taking the principles and turning them into reality.

C. Bev, from ALIGN, provides the following:

During my own de-cluttering process and the birthing of ALIGN, I discovered my unconscious limiting beliefs were keeping me stuck in my clutter! If that were true, I knew others were experiencing the same. My work began to evolve from simply helping people rid themselves of clutter to examine what lies under their clutter. By identifying unconscious limiting beliefs, people can begin the releasing process with a compassionate view of themselves and their clutter. This creates openings for transformation to occur.

I started to use different tools to facilitate the process: Tarot cards and essential oils. Tarot card images reflect subconscious thoughts and feelings of the person being read. This spurred me to develop Tarot spreads that examine issues underlying clutter. Images, rather than words, tap into the right brain enabling people to see their issues in an expanded way.

Clinical research has shown that essential oils can quickly raise the frequency of the human body, restoring it to its normal healthy level. I concluded that diffusing certain essential oils when de-cluttering would create a frequency that would support the releasing process.

D. Pam answered with the following:

The realization was a gradual process that Patricia has helped me unfold. She continues to help me believe in my own journey through encouragement and honesty. Also, I have received positive feedback from people who have taken part in my yoga classes. This has given me the green light that this is a viable business that fulfills a need in myself and others.

E. The response for myself and International Purpose (IP) are always:

Through my own deep inner work, over many years, my composite of unique skills and talents surfaced. I have the ability to help others:

1) Envision new work futures and identify their right fit;

2) Identify beliefs and fears that block progress; and

3) Surface and leverage their unique work composite of skills and talents.

I slowly began to realize that my innate talents could assist others to move through the same process toward the evolution of self and work. I began to realize that my needs were also their needs—they still are. My sense of wisdom, connection to a higher power and understanding of humanity, matched to what was going on in the world and marketplace, were very instrumental in assisting me to see the business case for my work.

Question #2: How did you determine the particular "niche" for your unique composite of skills and talents?

Ryta: Part of this started when I was volunteering with a winery and encountered people who wanted to learn more about wine. This got me thinking about this "need and desire" that was missing in the marketplace. I saw that people often felt intimidated by wines and this was a niche to address.

Traveling to California and experiencing the wine tasting done there made me realize that there is nothing like this in Pennsylvania, where I'm from. I called friends back home, described what I was doing and was told they felt like they were there themselves. I realized I could bring people into this process in a relaxing, enjoyable way.

What surfaced is a process I call edu-social—to educate people to wines in a social environment. I received a lot of compliments from others on this idea. I think the big thing is finding your niche, which doesn't have to be one met before.

I knew I could meet this need so I started by trial and error doing in-house wine-tastings. I started asking the next "right" questions: "How do I make this more meaningful?" "How can I service more people?"

Dave: My niche is contracting to firms with a wide range of problem situations brewing. Here my breadth and seniority become strengths, coupled with my natural adaptability. Through a lot of testing and introspection, I've learned that I fail when a situation gets too bounded by institution rules, management preferences or other artificial constraints. Conversely, I thrive in a situation where there is pressure and opportunity to improvise and push the current assumptions. I am at my best left on my own with some resources and a group of motivated or excited people who can gain improved work lives, new skills or recognition for making things work better.

Bev: At first I was willing to take any client who needed help de-cluttering. I attracted individuals so deeply enmeshed in their clutter that they weren't ready to take that first step. At one point I thought it would be beneficial to work with realtors. Their clients want to sell their homes and some of those clients have clutter. I thought I could work with the cluttered clients before home stagers arrive to prepare the house for sale. Conversations with a few realtors sharpened my focus. I wanted to help people transform—not just move their stuff.

It took repeated conversations with a colleague who specializes in branding to define my client base. This was when I came up with the term "create openings," which elaborated on the transformative process. By creating openings, a client is receptive to new ideas, opportunities and creativity—these represent forward movement and the antithesis of being stuck.

Pam: I focused on listing and exploring my skills and talents, capitalizing on the things that come somewhat effortlessly and naturally to me which include music, dance, rhythm, movement, digging deep spiritually and emotionally within myself, and how that translates to others.

IP: The niche for my work, in many ways, is people much like myself—those I can best relate to. Individuals who know they have greater work to do but are stuck in the old paradigm of work. My niche is working with small businesses, with a focus on social responsibility, who want to make a greater difference through their work, evolve themselves and gain a nice return.

I saw socially responsible entrepreneurs and small businesses as my market niche because:

1) I, personally, have always been intrigued by the work and businesses people develop;

2) Small businesses have the flexibility to change quickly—if they choose;

3) This segment of the marketplace is the fastest growing; and

4) Many small businesses know they need to change and are willing to spend the time, money and energy to do so.

Question #3: What deeper human needs does your service/product meet?

Ryta: The wine-tasting room itself will meet people's needs of belonging, to feel comfort and comfortable, as well as to be accepted—which builds their self-esteem and self-importance.

Dave: I tap into people's drive to make things better, to be creative, to apply skills and be valued or validated, and to step beyond the daily grind—to make work/business fun and rewarding.

Bev: In short, my service facilitates a client's need to be free, to express his/her creative self. By doing this, the client can get closer to identifying and acting on his/her life purpose.

Pam: People are hungry for connection and community. I want to provide a place where people can come together, where it is accepted and encouraged to take off not only your socks and shoes, but your masks as well. It is a chance to experience the divine through movement, prayer, song and meditation.

IP: The deeper needs that my service meets are the following:
1) A longing to reach a higher level of their own potential;
2) The need for more meaningful and purposeful work; and
3) The ability to leave the world a better place.

Question #4: How did you identify these needs?

Ryta: Patricia and I talked about this. I thought about what makes me want to go back to a certain retail establishment again and again. I talked to others about this, relative to the environment I create in my home and why they keep coming back.

Dave: I didn't identify it directly. Basically I found where I could serve after getting frustrated or fired. I have always sought out projects that are using new ideas or have some buzz about them or take place in a context somewhat unfamiliar to me. This has led me to do work for 60 different companies. While company cultures range widely in their type, people tend to have very similar motivations.

Bev: I had to de-clutter myself after my mother's death. It was a slow, sometimes tedious process. The experience I gained divesting myself of my own clutter enabled me to help others. I discovered others were struggling with their clutter and needed help.

Pam: Through my own needs. I discovered what I was longing for and I knew if I was longing for it so were others.

IP: The need became very apparent in myself and in others as I did my own work. The same needs kept showing up and repeating themselves. I could no longer ignore them.

B-2. Matching Your Work Purpose to the Need(s) in the Marketplace – Here's the Challenge:

Of course, it's now your turn to answer these questions. Do take the time you need.

Thank you,
Patricia

1. How did you realize that your unique skills could be used as part of "new" work or business in the marketplace?

2. How did you determine the particular "niche" for your unique composite of skills and talents?

3. What deeper human needs does your service/product meet?

4. How did you identity these needs?

B-3. Packaging & Presenting Your Purpose as Viable & Sustainable

In order to directly meet the deeper needs you identified in the marketplace, form and structure is the next step. The packaging and the presentation needs to be developed to attract your audience. The value needs to be extremely clear.

When thinking of packaging, here are some points to consider:

> *The form and structure your work/business takes is unique to you.*

✦ *It may "look" like a service/product that already exists, but its essence is based on what you bring to the table.*

> *It is a reflection of a need in the marketplace.*

✦ *It leverages all that you want to bring forth through your work.*

✦ *It's of your making.*

As I've always said, I've never seen a "purpose" that wasn't needed in the marketplace. There is great need in the world for your work, and it is up to you to package it in a form that your audience can relate to and that has meaning and purpose for them. Then and only then can they see the value and be willing to pay the price.

Additional points to consider about packaging:

✦ *It needs to be flexible so it can change and evolve with the deeper needs in the marketplace.*

✦ *Being attractive and inviting is key.*

> *Whenever possible, make it holistic in nature so it addresses mind, body and spirit, which will give it a broader meaning and greater value.*

> *Throw in a fun aspect and you will have a winner.*

When presenting something new in terms of an idea or concept, a good place to start is with an offering through which your audience can gain a sense of your service or product at a reasonable price. Once the value is recognized, then a larger offering can be presented that makes a greater difference and can give you a larger return.

You must then keep current with your evolving audience and marketplace. Technology, changing values, varying generational needs are just a few of the variables that need constant focus.

(Note: You may want to refer back to the end of Tool 2 to look at the work you did on your mind-map and brainstorming on matching you to the marketplace. This section can offer clues to assist you here.)

The following are again examples from Ryta, Dave, Bev, Pam and myself.

Question #1: How did you determine the appropriate "packaging" for your work to present and sell it to others?

Ryta: Once I got the idea that I wanted to be in the wine/food/social business, I began to listen more intently to those I would encounter in these areas. Through my work with both a PA winery and a distributor, I kept hearing similar things about people's desires to know more about wine. They wanted to learn more and enjoy the experience. They wanted wine to be fun, not work.

Dave: The key to packaging is engaging the customer without screaming a message. One learns a lot from what does not work. I present my proposals as a solution to a client-specific or industry problem. Clients want to know what you can do for them and why they should believe you (credibility). There is a delicate balance between being simple and being too clever or mysterious. My recent tagline was "Inventory-Market Harmony." Virtually all manufacturing or distribution companies face the problems of having inventory and service levels out of sync with the market. Selling a solution involves a series of conversations that begins with asking questions and proceeds to selling an analysis or diagnostic of the situation and opportunity assessment. Getting the chance to do this requires listening, qualifying that the client would do a project and can afford to, and providing an offer they cannot refuse. If you talk benefits such as reducing inventories or improving customer service, there is lots of room for a forward-looking conversation.

Bev: I have discovered that the mere mention of "clutter" evokes a reaction. Until recently I introduced myself as a declutterer and then talked about the transformative nature of my work. This seemed sexy because of the titter it evoked, but as my work evolved, mentioning clutter first and transformation second didn't feel right. I have revised my introduction so that it addresses the transformative nature of my work up front.

Pam: I am still in the process of fine-tuning this. It is an ongoing evolution. I've done several yoga classes at my church, and I continue to refine and grow.

IP: Internally, I looked at the type of service that matched my experience, knowledge and passions. Externally, I looked at what entrepreneurs and small business owners were missing and longing for in their day-to-day business and how my own work purpose could address these needs. I also looked at basic human nature and how people were evolving. The most apparent needs I saw were for greater community, partnering with like-minded people, expanding their potential, and making a greater difference through their work and, in turn, gaining a better return. These factors evolved into an entrepreneurial group called Purposeful Business Circles, described further in my next few replies.

Question #2: What is your service/product?

Ryta: Provide a wine experience that is unique to each person, giving them something regardless of their level of knowledge. It's an experience where individuals grow and learn as they have fun doing it.

Dave: I impose a concept onto a problem supply chain situation and create a practical way to make it work. Often this involves tuning the production and distribution systems to customer demand patterns. We let customers "pull" product from the end of the system and tune it to provide product there at the lowest cost. I work toward maximizing customer service and minimizing the cost of service. I carry in a construct that the client may be missing or has not fully applied and overlay that on their situation to improve their business.

Bev: I offer a variety of services:

a) Tele-classes that help people de-clutter independently and at the same time require accountability
b) Class: "Clutter is Spiritual Business"—a four-week (8-hour) class that examines what lies under one's clutter
c) De-cluttering consultation/coaching in an individual's home (usually in 2- or 3-hour sessions)
d) Tarot readings that can focus on clutter or general life issues
e) Instruction on essential oils, how they are used and what oils are beneficial for specific purposes.

Pam: I lead yoga classes. Yoga, for me, is a platform to introduce not only the physical postures of yoga but also prayer and meditation. The class is a place to nurture our acts of kindness in the world, kindness to ourselves, other people, animals and the environment.

IP: An enlightened business group called Purposeful Business Circles (PBC). This model and process is based on the belief that our life purpose can be transformed into a thriving business; that the collective model is one that can exponentially assist us to evolve; and that personal growth directly impacts business growth.

Question #3: What are you doing to keep your service/product viable and sustainable now and into the future?

Ryta: It's very important for me to keep current on trends such as what's hot in the wine and food industry. What are people gravitating toward? What makes a business sustainable? I look at established businesses and find out how they have stayed in business so long. Also, I have to be flexible and provide my service/product in a consistent manner.

Dave: The next phase will be to look at unfulfilled needs and problems and create the products and services to meet them. This part of the supply chain starts in the minds of the customer and the supplier. The trick in innovation is that people often cannot put their finger on exactly what they would want to improve, but know it when they see it.

I am working toward building a process to identify relevant trends and needs in the marketplace, make your unique product/service concrete and package it in a way that people can buy. To get there will involve talking to the people and markets I want to serve.

Bev: ALIGN reflects my own spiritual growth and development. I continue to broaden my spiritual awareness and understanding by immersing myself in the teachings of and conversing with like-minded people. As I do this I get ideas which, I believe, are divinely inspired. These ideas cause me to change my approach and explore new areas of discovery. No matter what happens, I learn from these changes. Client feedback gives me valuable information as well.

Pam: I keep myself inspired, learning and growing. I attend workshops and continue to nurture my own daily meditation and yoga practice. Yoga has been around for many, many years and will continue to thrive and grow.

IP: Staying viable and sustainable into the future will require courage, straight thinking and purposeful action. It will require a service/product that is evolutionary in nature so that the service evolves as it evolves those it serves.

Some of the new actions and systems being developed are:

1) A detailed global vision and plan to develop PBCs worldwide as an enlightened business model and way of working that networks these groups around the world.

2) An outside accountability system of select individuals I'm calling an Outer Circle. This Circle will help me stay on track with executing our vision and plan.

3) A program to train others to assist and facilitate the PBCs—locally and worldwide.

4) Partnerships with international development firms to both implement PBCs within their firms and partner with them to implement PBCs in other countries.

B-3. Packaging & Presenting Your Purpose as Viable & Sustainable – Here's the <u>Challenge</u>:

Time and thought are needed for the following. Given your situation, you can answer in the present tense or future. Do your best, and, if needed, come back to this section later. Remember that clarity comes over time.

Thanks for your continued work,
Patricia

1. What will it take to determine the appropriate "packaging" for your work to present and sell it to others?

2. What is your service/product? (Define this to the best of your ability.)

3. What will you do to keep your service/product viable and sustainable now and into the future?

C. Building Relationships –
Attracting the Right Audience

Today's marketplace is unique, just like your offering. It is ever-changing and evolving. Because of this your marketing approach and mindset need to be more flexible, as well as more personal. As mentioned before, you need to "touch" your audience at a deep level, for only then will they be called to purchase what you have to offer.

Once you know the emotional needs your service/product addresses, you can then start building the "right" relationships and determining the marketing approach best suited to address these needs.

Marketing and selling are not what they used to be. It is not so much about the advertising dollars, the number of calls made or your quota. It is about the relationships created, the knowledge and wisdom shared, and the difference you are making in people's lives. It's about learning how to "be" your work, which then attracts others to it.

Because of the often new and different nature of purposeful work, part of your marketing may actually be education. Your service/product may address a need that your audience doesn't realize they have. In cases like this, the first step is to both increase awareness and create comfort.

A technique I naturally use when I'm meeting people for the first time is to "help them on the spot" by introducing myself and asking them a question about themselves. I then listen very intently and follow up with a question that takes what they have said to a deeper level. This usually helps them see their situation from a different perspective and see that they have more choices than they realize.

We can all help people on the spot by being and demonstrating our purpose at all times. This allows us to then demonstrate the power of our work in the world.

All of the above demands that we present ourselves and our work to many people in many different ways and circumstances. I have another term for this: "being out and about"—in the marketplace and in the community (more to come later on this technique).

This section just touches the surface in terms of these topics. You will want to read the following sub-sections and do the Challenges. As you work on this section, you will begin to see, in a deeper way, the business case for your purpose.

C-1. IDENTIFYING YOUR "IDEAL" AUDIENCE

The first thing you must determine are the characteristics of your "ideal" audience. If you start here you will attract the clients that best fit your service or product. Often, when starting a new business, people believe that their offering is so universal and of such value that everyone will want it. Not so. Don't get fooled into believing that you can please everyone all the time because this will disperse your energy and time in too many directions. You need to focus on the precise characteristics of your particular audience and then market to this composite.

The more specific you can be in identifying your market "niche" the better. This then makes the attraction and marketing process easy. Some of this work you have already done in the last section on identifying needs. Additional areas to explore are:

+ *Where their pain and/or passion is*
+ *What they value and believe in*
+ *Where they go for information they need*
+ *What volunteer work they do*
+ *What types of networking events they attend*
+ *What social media they utilize*

It's now your turn and time to take the lead; add additional areas you would like to explore.

+
+
+
+

The following responses, from others like yourself, will definitely help in defining your ideal client. Be sure to write your answers in the Challenge section.

Question #1: What are some of the characteristics of your "ideal" audience?

Ryta. The obvious one is someone who wants to learn more about wine. These people can be novices to experts. As long as they are open-minded and willing to learn, then they are my clients. I feel strongly about supporting PA wines, which we will be serving. These wines don't have the best reputation, so people will need to be willing to explore these wines. I understand what it has taken for people to open their wineries and how really good they are.

Dave: The answers are situational in nature. Businesses where:

+ There is a clear problem with a deadline or market with a deadline or consequence for not solving it.
+ Obvious solutions or software have bogged down.
+ Management and the client have let go of the idea that they already know what needs to be done—else it would be done already.
+ Individuals are hiding in the bureaucracy and are not adding value. Some of them want the work itself to go better.
+ Company seems "fine" except that results are lagging and a next step is not clear.
+ There is a low tolerance for expensive, jargon-laden approaches common to big consulting firms.

Bev: Clients open to change and who want to transform. The characteristics are:

+ Disgruntled about their clutter and can't move it by themselves;
+ Ready for change and recognize that clutter is part of the problem;
+ Seek help to move their clutter and in the process realize that clutter is a symptom of a much larger issue—their spirituality; and

✦ Seek structure and accountability when they de-clutter because otherwise they will get distracted, discouraged and defeated.

Pam: Kind, open minded, a willingness to learn, a sense of humility, a desire to make a difference in this world not only for ourselves but for the good of other people, animals and the environment.

IP: I've chosen to list a set of demographics and psychographics:

✦ Entrepreneurs and small business owners who have been in business for at least two to three years or previously ran an established business.
✦ A service business rather than a product-oriented one.
✦ Participate in professional/personal development work.
✦ Know the benefit of spending the time and money on themselves and their business.
✦ Belong to and participate in professional associations in their field.
✦ Want to make a difference through their work.
✦ Spiritual and life-long learners.
✦ Looking to grow their businesses, make a greater impact, as they increase revenue.
✦ Currently feel stuck, aren't making progress, and/or feel as if they are repeating the past.
✦ Are "green" and socially responsible.
✦ Have a good network from which they can refer others.
✦ Realize that they might be getting in their own way and that ultimately it is up to them to first create the change within themselves.

C-1. Identifying Your "Ideal" Audience – Here's the Challenge:

The better you can clearly define your ideal audience, the more successful you will be. Your work is not for everyone, but for a select group who will embrace and honor what you have to offer.

Thanks,
Patricia

1. Refer back to the beginning of this section to explore the areas on identifying your ideal audience. What are some of the characteristics of your "ideal" audience?

C-2. Your Attraction & Marketing Strategy

The attraction and marketing processes are distinct and yet overlapping. Marketing is the action-oriented piece, while attraction is energetic in nature.

Attracting clients, in very simple terms, is the way of energetically pulling people to your work/business. It is the harder of the two because it demands that you "be" a clean and clear mirror for your audience. It demands that you constantly do your homework around living a consciously conscious life, clear of the blocks that limit your purpose in the world.

The concept of the Law of Attraction has recently come to light through the work of *The Secret* by Rhonda Byrne and *The Missing Secret* by Joe Vitale. Matthew Fox actually stated it quite clearly years ago in his book *The Re-Invention of Work*, in which he said that we play too small with visions that aren't large enough. He said the larger the vision, the more it will be a magnet—a self-motivator for you and an attractor for others.

The good news is that, by working on the Seven Evolutionary Tools, you have been doing lots of self-development. Your ability to attract clients has been honed, and you are ahead of the game.

Marketing is the concrete way to get your business message out to your audience. It is a targeted approach to disseminating information about your work. It may look like crafting ways to pull people to your website, blogging in a way that provides valued information, and/or networking with others that serve the same audience.

Effective marketing happens when it is a campaign of ongoing activities that consistently reaches your ideal client. Questions to ask yourself are:

1. What professional groups, associations or networks do I need to join? Within these groups, are there committees

or special-interest groups that I can participate in to build deeper relationships?

2. What on-line social networks are best for my marketing effort?

3. How much time and money do I need to and want to spend on marketing?

(Your turn to add a couple of your own.)

4.

5.

6.

In terms of attracting clients, I wanted to share what I tend to do. I take a two-prong approach of staying clear with myself and holding the space and container for this work. Examples are:

1. Meditating every morning to quiet my mind and listen for higher guidance.

2. Doing deeply healing work on myself to clear my internal blocks and emotional holdings.

3. Being helpful to others and showing I care.

4. Visualizing people coming into this work, the benefit they will gain, the fun they have and progress they will make.

5. Maintaining a positive attitude and not giving energy to my negative self-talk.

6. Staying centered and grounded in what I know and do.

7. Having faith "without a doubt" that I'm doing my purpose.

8. Plenty of self-care and balance in life and work—an ongoing challenge.

My marketing efforts are defined in the following section.

Question #1: What are some of the elements of your marketing campaign?

Ryta: I started by doing in-home wine tasting to build a client base. I worked to increase my visibility by attending functions in the wine industry and joining relevant business groups. I identified key constituent groups and started networking.

Also, it was key to pick the right location for the business, just tell people, have a marketing plan and, lastly, just keeping it all "real."

Dave: I am looking for firms with projects where I can excel and using that to get in front of them for an interview. I talk about their challenges and solutions and what I have developed in similar circumstances. They have to envision the fit themselves, and once this happens, they begin to think of additional places I might be of value. The best approach is when you ask a question and provide an example of how you answered that question in the past, working your skills and techniques into it.

I would like to change this by writing a book or having a productized solution that exposes more people to my unique ideas.

Bev: I do and have the following to market to clients:

1. Website: www.alignyourlife.net
2. E-newsletter: Align Your Life as well as blogging
3. Postcards and fliers (individually distributed and posted on bulletin boards)
4. Asking for referrals
5. Networking with my ideal audience
6. Writing articles
7. Future endeavors: E-book, speaking engagements, social media like Facebook and LinkedIn

Pam: I am communicating with people through one-on-one and group talks, creating flyers and business cards and, just new in the works, marketing a yoga DVD to help promote health ministry through a local parish nurse organization.

IP: My marketing campaign is focused on getting information about my work into the minds and hands of the "right" audience. I am doing this by:

1. Networking with groups that attract my audience and referral base,
2. Inviting individuals to "experience" the Purposeful Business Circles,
3. Staying connected to my database of entrepreneurs and small business owners through various online communications such as my monthly newsletter
4. Developing myself as more of an authority in this field through speaking engagements and publishing.

"The value of a product or service changes not just according to its marketing window but according to the consumer's own immediate future."

– "Visionary's Handbook: Nine Paradoxes That Will Shape the Future of Your Business"

C-2. YOUR ATTRACTION & MARKETING STRATEGY – HERE'S THE PURPOSEFUL <u>CHALLENGE</u>:

The clearer you can be with your responses, the better. These questions may take time to gain the clarity needed, so do as much as you can. You will note that I added a second question. Again, if needed, do these in a couple of sittings.

Remember how close you are to manifesting your purpose,
Patricia

1. What are some of the elements of your marketing campaign?

2. How are you "being" and what are you doing to attract clients?

C-3. Re-defining Selling

We are always selling. We sell our ideas, our wants and desires, and our perception of the world. We help others see the benefit of what we believe. So why do we shy away from the thought of "selling" our work.

For some this feels like literally giving away their soul and succumbing to something beneath them. Somehow we think we are above this—like our work should sell itself. Yes and no.

Yes, we can visualize the results we want and attract clients as we become our work. But given that we live in middle-ground, the space between heaven and earth, we need to also sell in some intentional ways.

The thought of selling is so fearful to some that it keeps potential entrepreneurs out of the marketplace. They want to start their own business but in the same breathe say, "But, I can't sell."

I say, yes, you can. The way I see it, the key to selling is to determine the "right" questions that enable others to surface the following:

+ *Their current need for what you have to offer,*
+ *How your offering can relieve their pain and/or enable their passion,*
+ *The deeper need your work addresses,*
+ *The benefits they will receive in spending the time and money, and*
+ *How easy it is to take the first step towards purchasing your service/ product.*

The goal is to have them sell themselves by identifying the value added that your service or product brings to their life and work.

If you truly believe that what you have to offer will greatly improve the lives and work of others and that without your work they will miss that opportunity—then you have a winner.

See what others have to say in terms of techniques to use in selling. (You will find some overlap here between marketing and selling.)

Question #1: What types of techniques do you use to sell to your prospects?

Ryta:
1. Incentives to purchase.
2. "Try free" technique—I offer three wines to taste; usually I can hit the right taste, and they buy at least one of these.
3. Creating fun around the product.
4. Highlighting the social and health benefits of wine.
5. Educating people on what wines are best with what foods; e.g., sweet wine and ice cream.
6. First learning something about the client to then best meet their needs.
7. Always having something new and interesting for people to experience—e.g., changing stock seasonally.
8. Bringing them back for something more than that one experience—seasonal events that are different and that you can expect to be good.
9. Being consistent.

Dave:
1. Case studies of similar problems solved.
2. Free analysis to assess the situation.
3. Clarify the buying process, the decision-makers, and whether a budget or signing authority exists within the team I am presenting to.
4. Before and after results summaries.

Bev:
1. I tell my own story with clutter.
2. I offer different ways of getting my service: Tele-classes, classes, one-on-one consultation.
3. If clients like the first three-hour consultation, I offer a package rate for additional sessions.

Pam: By being honest, kind, enthusiastic and authentic. Allowing people to try an introductory class to see if this may be something that they would like to pursue.

IP: The following are a few examples of what I do:
1. Ask a lot of questions to get prospects to talk about their needs.
2. Give examples of how others have benefited.
3. Offer a first step such as an Initial Consultation or attending a Purposeful Business Circle Half-Day Experience.
4. Show genuine caring for them and their issues.
5. Education them to the exact nature of the work.
6. Ask about their next right step.

C-3. RE-DEFINING SELLING –
HERE'S THE <u>CHALLENGE</u>:

As with Ryta, this may be a future action for you. Now is a good time to give it some thought. Be creative, put yourself in your client's shoes and write all that comes up—no right or wrong to this.

Your confidence and courage is laudable,
Patricia

1. What types of techniques do you or can you use to sell to your prospects?

D. STRATEGICALLY CREATING FROM THE FUTURE

In order to develop work and business that will enable new futures, you must be clear on the future you want to create and your part in doing so. This is where your purpose, vision and mission statements play a strategic role. Your purpose statement needs to "be" part and parcel of who you are every day. Your vision and mission need to be at your fingertips and used as references in decision making and planning.

This is also where everything from Tools 1 through 6 needs to consciously surface to be by your side. You will truly realize that the new tools and habits you have developed was time well spent.

Creating this new future requires that your daily actions be based on your future of choice while you stay focused on the present. This will allow the next "right" decision and step to be taken. This happens when you develop action steps that are strategically mission-based.

Ultimately, your daily, weekly and monthly decisions need to consider all of the above. As you focus and incorporate these, they become a natural offshoot of who you are. Over time this process will become easy and integrated.

D-1. STRATEGICALLY PLANNING THE FUTURE

Strategically planning means taking a more holistic and global approach. This means considering more expansive elements in your own planning process. Elements like:

1. How to develop a sustainable impact,
2. Determining price points for your service/product that denote value on many levels, and
3. Leveraging uniqueness that meets multiple needs—needs of your client, their client, the community and even the world, and certainly your needs as well.

This process of strategic planning often takes more reflection, and this can be time consuming. It is best done with others who are like-minded to broaden the input and results.

The following questions came to the surface only in retrospect—where many great questions come from. Therefore, you will find only two examples, from Dave and myself.

Question #1: What will it take to keep your purpose, vision and mission statements in front of you, as a key resource, as you plan your work?

Dave: Print them out. Post them where I can see them each day. Ask how my purpose, vision and mission apply to each day and situation I face. Understand my unique strengths and play them rather than adapt to patterns imposed socially by those around me or to whom I report. Honor the strengths and missions of others. Playing to their strengths provides an opportunity for them to play to mine. "Contract" for this as much as possible with those with whom I work. Plan to use my strengths and supplement my gaps with the strengths of others to meet goals.

IP: It will literally take me putting these three statements "in front of my face" so I can refer to them weekly as I do my planning. I will also share these with my team.

Question #2: How do you best keep one foot in the present and one in the future of choice as you develop actions that represent both?

Dave: This can be difficult when facing the practical reality of making a living with the best available present work option. By viewing current work as building toward future work, one's actions can represent both. For me, my goal to innovate a new product start-up is led by working in a new product start-up. Today is the real-life case study for tomorrow. An analogy is that this is an apprenticeship, even being the "sorcerer's apprentice." The apprentice knows for a fact that he/she will one day be the practitioner.

IP: I plan for the week by referring to what I stated above. I also daily aim to stay in the present and be observant of what comes up. As one of my coaches and I have discussed, I have to be careful not to let my "productivity gene" take over. When it does, my intuition takes a back seat.

Question #3: What does actualizing your mission statement look like?

Dave: My mission, as best I can currently state it, is to connect people with concepts to manifest improvements in life. All my work has aligned with this. At this phase of my career, I see the challenge in the manifest element. As an employee and consultant, my role has been to manifest in the context of my employer or client's needs, using a known concept. My future manifesting, as I currently see it, is to engage in problem-finding and discovery, bringing to bear the right concept manifestation to solve the need. Then I would drive the sequence end-to-end, in which I have previously played various parts.

IP: For me it:

✦ Looks like partnering and teaming with many like-minded individuals with unique skills that complement and add value to mine;

✦ Means being very healthy in mind, body, emotions and spirit;

✦ Means doing more of my work using different formats;

◆ Looks like a wonderful office space in a big house;

✦ Means letting go of control, being willing to ask for help, and realizing that the GEPO method, "good enough push on," is the only way to go.

For this last question, Ryta and Bev also contributed.

Question #4: What are the key strategies for the future that you want to create?

Ryta: My goals for the future include multiple locations of the Naked Grape to reach more people and create unique interactions not common in the hospitality industry. I want people to know what I have known for years, that wine and food can be a perfect combination from which to build friendships, business relationships and, most of all, respect for each other.

My little corner of "entrepreneurship" will be a place where our business is known for welcoming all and finding common ground between people. I am creating in a space that can be "reproduced" in its feel and ambience. I am developing guidelines for every practice within the business that can be used in future locations and making sure that constant assessment is an integral part of everything we do.

From a pragmatic standpoint, my future goal is to have a business that is thriving financially so it supports both my husband and me in a moderately comfortable lifestyle. It's not about reaching for the brass ring of materialism but about our business impacting others in a positive way and perhaps changing the way others view life. Given this, we are trying to maintain our budget, start small and slow to build our business as it is ready, not forcing it and us into financial difficulties. Our plan is fiscally conservative, which we aim to stick to despite the temptation to "go big" at the outset. Daily I try to be mindful of what my dream was, is and will be, and keep reminding myself that despite difficulties, I am the creator of my own destiny.

Dave: I am working to create "context-generating" situations where I understand the problems facing a market in enough detail to bring in a new perspective and deliberate creativity to work out a novel, value-creating solution. The starting point is building a relationship with one person who lives in the context, winning their trust and listening to what they face. There are a number of models for developing the understanding from market analysis to scientific observation and from surveys to focus groups and from brainstorming to experimentation.

Bev: Become more visible in the marketplace through the following:
1. Identify and secure speaking opportunities
2. Schedule tele-classes on a regular basis
3. Write and submit articles for publication
4. Expand my database for e-newsletters
5. Write a regularly scheduled e-newsletter
6. Revise my website to attract the appropriate traffic
7. Create new courses

IP: I know I can't do this business alone; therefore, one of my strategies is to develop key relationships and partners. I now realize that this can happen on many levels. One that currently hits home is to work more closely with my assistant, who happens to be my sister, and have her get more involved in the business. This can start by sharing with her the strategic plan for the business and asking her about the part she is interested in playing now and over the next few years. We also need to discuss staying out of sister-mode, as I call it, when she and I make remarks that work against the greater goals for us and the business.

D-1. Strategically Planning the Future – Here's the Challenge:

Give yourself plenty of reflective quiet time to answer the following questions. Your responses are key to your strategic planning. Don't forget to use your journal.

Thanks,
Patricia

1. What will it take to keep your purpose, vision and mission statements in front of you, as a key resource, as you plan your work?

2. How do you or will you best keep one foot in the present and one in the future of choice as you develop your actions that represent both?

3. What does actualizing your mission statement look like?

4. What are the key strategies for the future that you want to create?

D-2. DAILY ACTIVITIES IN THE HERE & NOW

Staying in the present, calm and collected, is key to success in these challenging economic times. In this state you can focus on the future of choice and act accordingly.

The key question to be asking ourselves and working toward on a daily basis is, What are the actions today that will most seed the future of choice? The answer to this question then helps determine the plans for each day.

It goes back to keeping one foot in the present and one foot in the future. Learning and cultivating this skill will serve you well.

Question: What does or will your day-to-day reality look like to seed your future of choice?

Ryta: My days start fairly early as I head into the restaurant to open up, prepare the space, assist the chef and gear up for a daily "team" meeting. A brief one with the staff to be sure we iron out any glitches; listen to what they see, hear, need; and make sure they know they are appreciated. I handle multiple phone calls and float between the tables to use my expertise in assisting clients above and beyond what our team will be doing. In slow times, I clean bathrooms, sweep floors, assist the chef and plan the promotion of our business through events, public relations and media contact. Midway through the workday, I check our numbers to see where we are with income and motivate as necessary. When the second shift comes in, we meet. At the end of the day, I assist the chef and staff with clean up, check/update inventory, assess what we did that day, plan for the next day and run financial reports for the day's activities. When the door closes behind me, I want to have made a difference, be prepared for the next day and feel great, for I'm living my dream!

Dave: My day-to-day reality consists of a day job and a dream job that are slowly coming closer together and will hopefully be one in the same. My current day job consists of consulting to enable customers and our robots to best work together. Here is where I focus on building and using my skills and experience to make my best contribution and to bring in my unique perspective. I build one client relationship at a time, listen to their problems and goals and do analysis to see what will work. Then, I work with the right member of the client to sell the idea and propose a new way of doing things. I read within my field of manufacturing/distribution systems and specific industries like food and retailing to see what problems are being discussed or what new ideas are being pushed.

My dream job is working to build a new product business. The challenge is to get out of the clouds or books and into the contexts I mentioned above. I am resolved to form a group of fellow explorers and conduct one-on-one interviews to drill into some specific markets.

Bev: For more than two years I made myself available whenever my clients needed me. I would squeeze whatever time remained for thinking, planning, creating and writing. This prevented me from spending quality time to develop my business. Recently I have changed this pattern. I schedule either one full day or a morning and an afternoon of each week for course development, e-newsletters, writing articles and other activities.

I see clients in either the morning or the afternoon, whatever works for the two of us. I work with clients in their home during a 2- or 3-hour consultation. Travel time usually includes another hour. I have also worked on weekends for those clients who have full-time jobs and are not available during the working hours of the week.

Pam: Day-to-day reality requires discipline to continue my daily morning yoga practice. I also set aside time for business-related work (phone calls, advertising and class planning). I am married, have a six-year-old child and two dogs and am very active in all aspects of life, including my daughter's activities, as well as volunteering for the local animal shelter and being very active in my church. Life is full and discipline and persistence seem to be my challenges, but they are also the key to moving forward with my life's mission.

IP: Every day is different, but it always starts out the same with meditating and reading from an inspirational book as well as taking a walk. This both focuses me on the higher order of my life and work and grounds me in the realities of life.

Knowing that I love ideas and "playing in the ethers" causes me to put order into every day to both feel and be accomplished. I tend to leave the mornings for business development and writing, as well as for marketing calls. The afternoons are then time for individual GuideWork/Coaching and small business clients, working with my assistant, lunch meetings, etc. Early evening will sometimes involve attending a networking event or paying bills. I always plan by the week, in blocks of time.

My goal is always to create a balanced week. For me, being an extrovert and spending too much time alone can leave me a bit empty. This I'm actively changing.

D-2. Daily Activities in the Here & Now – Here's the Challenge:

This response actually shouldn't take too long. (I'm sure this isn't the first time I've said this!)

Have fun,
Patricia

1. What does or will your day-to-day reality look like when you seed your future of choice?

D-3. Creating Your Service/Product as a Means to Evolution

Your work can be your teacher—a very different definition than is the norm. The business of today is the business of learning from life. You may have heard the saying "We teach what we need to learn best" as we also "Teach best from our own experience."

When your work/business is rooted in your life experience, the end result can't help but be successful because you have lived it.

The next three questions are meant to pull from deep within you. Now is the time to let your work be your teacher.

Question #1: What are some of the specific things you have learned about yourself, life and/or the world of work by using the Seven Evolutionary Tools?

Ryta: About myself, I've learned that I'm capable of almost anything I want to do. I've had to "relearn" this. I did this as a child but lost this when I worked at the university. I learned that what makes me tick is to impact the lives of others. I just am an entrepreneur. Once I got out of the job mind-set I started to realize that doing something on my own is like oxygen for me.

Also, when I looked at my gene pool I realized that being an entrepreneur is very prevalent in my family and that it all made sense. As I have been doing this, many of my friends and acquaintances have said they wish they could be freer to do the same. The world of work is actually boundless.

Dave: I've learned to just get started. You don't need what you learned or studied, but it will help you as you deal with the real world. This too shall pass: this job, this problem, this management, etc. Some enemies are not really intentional enemies, just very self-centered or slightly sociopathic people. Just avoid them or go around them. Otherwise, load yourself with lots of data.

Let your ideas ripen before you share them (for you extroverts out there). Keep your idea a secret from anyone who would not fully support it, especially close relationships, until you have momentum behind it.

Character traits like sincerity, enthusiasm, positive attitude and resilience still reach fellow humans. Those traits like cynicism, criticism, stereotyping and whining attract the wrong audience and eventually trip you up.

People rally around the hope that a new idea, backed by sound thinking and analysis, can make their work lives better. Ideas need a champion, not just the person selling it.

Bev: Life is delicious. It is up to me to see it that way and to make it so. Our world is always changing. We can choose to go with the flow or not. Many are stuck in their past, fearing the future and the change it may mean for their life. By holding onto the past and resisting the present and its opportunities, they suffer consequences. They literally get stiff, set in their ways and resistant.

In extreme circumstances, this decision leads to isolation—not only disconnected from others but disconnected from one's spiritual self. We forget we have a life purpose and we're here to implement it. Every moment can be an opportunity to experience a new adventure, a new idea, a new person. This attachment to the past holds us back from experiencing the deliciousness of each new moment.

Pam: I have learned that I have not been naturally motivated by money and I continue to explore the reasons why. I am creating a balance between charity and making money. I am evolving and working on getting comfortable in a businesswoman's hat.

IP: I have learned how we have so much of life and work all backwards. We have been made to believe that the physical world is the basis from which everything is determined and judged. How misguided we have been. In actuality our inner world, higher guidance and belief in ourselves are the true foundation.

I've learned more than I could have ever imagined. It feels like I've evolved many lifetimes. I get teary eyed as I recognize this for the hundredth time. This is my calling, without a doubt.

I do sometimes wonder how I got here, and at the same time I do know at least part of the answer. I got here as a way to overcome fear, control and ego—as I also got here out of passion, belief in a better world and our ability as human beings to evolve.

Question #2: From a place of self-actualization, how is your work helping others transcend so they can also experience self-actualization?

Dave: Valuing others and myself in our strengths and minimizing the competition and jealousy that comes within and between organizations strengthens everyone in reaching their mission. The other tension is the reality of dealing with power and money in taking next steps to reaching our self-actualization. Realities may provide temporary setbacks or blockages, but new paths can emerge by being present to the lessons of the present with an eye toward our future. For me, this usually means finding a new project, founding a new company or networking my current story as it has evolved.

IP: More than anything else, I help people get out of their own way. I guide people to their truth, and in so doing they self-actualize on their own accord. I help them see the innate beauty of themselves. This happens as I help others peel away what's on the surface so they can own their highest potential.

I am reminded of the words of my friend Ishwar, who recently passed: "Your success is my success." These words are of great comfort and support for us all.

D-3. Creating Your Service/Product as a Means to Evolution – Here's the Challenge:

This is the last Challenge. Complete it as you continue to put into action the next "right" step.

Thank you so very much for all your work,
Patricia

1. What are some of the specific things you have learned about yourself, life and/or the world of work by using the Seven Evolutionary Tools?

2. From a place of self-actualization, how is your work helping others transcend so they can also experience self-actualization?

APPENDIX

BEING A PART OF THE NEW WORK/BUSINESS EVOLUTION

As I write this I both smile and cry. The smile is one of pleasure and the tears are ones of joy. I am on this path with you, and I am deeply touched by the process. I find myself having conversations and wondering who is doing the talking. My mind hasn't completely transitioned to understand and accept this newly claimed power of my soul. My soul and my heart are now doing the talking. This is of tremendous comfort for a person who has been mastered by the head for so long. My knowing around the power of this work has reached a new level. It is work that people need, want and are longing for. It is the truth about our work as purpose in the world. Together we can thrive.

A. You Are the Future

"Events don't write the future. Events are given…
What isn't given is how we react to unknowable and
unpredictable events as they arrive. It's the response,
not the events, that determines both our future and our
satisfaction in the present with the future we expect."
– "The Visionary's Handbook"

You have come a long way, through many peaks and valleys, to make it to this point—job well done. As you read the Appendix, there are only a few additional points to be made—for you and me alike.

It's time to "model" the model of your new work future. Who you are in the world is a daily reflection of all the work you've done—on yourself, that is. At the same time it is a manifestation of your purpose in the world. You have developed as a power to be reckoned with, and it's now time to take your rightful place. Seeing this and accepting it are key, not in an egotistical way but from a sense of humility. It is necessary to be humble to keep your new-found power, for it will be quickly taken from those who abuse it.

Power is now redefined. Power as empowered, enabled, confident, wise, mature and humble. Being the new leader and the voice of reason will guide others to you. This new definition holds a valued and healthy perspective as we evolve into more enlightened work.

It's time to unveil "all" that you are to the world. This often requires a shift in self-image and internal perspective. It is time to mature into all that you are and be known. As you start hearing yourself talking anew with more self-assuredness, you may wonder who is doing the speaking. Your heart and soul are now partnering with the mind. This will bring a holistic approach to all you do. It's observing yourself from the outside in and marveling at what you see, only now it's also what you hear.

You are at yet another point of no return. Please don't take this lightly, for your work is vital at this time in the evolution of human kind. You have a new world to create—not a small task. At long last, the future can and will be of your making. As you build from all that you have learned and all that you are, the work world will shift—it has no choice. The world is in the midst of an awakening, and humankind is more evolved. You ARE ready for your part.

As a check against your progress, I'd like you to take a minute and re-take the Purpose Questionnaire as a post-evaluation to see how far you have come. Stop and respond to the questions on the next page.

Just a quick reminder to take good care of yourself as you move out into the world. This is actually more important than ever, for you need to be healthy in mind, body and spirit. In order to withstand the winds of change, the naysayers and your own fleeting negative self-talk, you must be healthy—maybe healthier than ever before. If you don't have a daily meditation program, regular body work, healthy eating habits and regular exercise, then start now. This is actually not a choice but a requirement to move forward in a dynamic way. These practices will enable internal energy to propel you and your work. Please don't skimp on this one.

Some questions to contemplate based on this section:

+ *What does having a greater presence and impact mean to you?*
+ *How do you position yourself in your business community as a leader with wisdom?*
+ *How do you strategically increase your visibility so the "right" people recognize your value-added?*
+ *How do you prepare yourself for busier times, maybe working with a larger audience?*
+ *Who might be the ideal assistant?*
+ *What is the benefit of having a regular meditation practice, getting regular body work and eating healthy food? Which of these do you need to improve now?*

Take the Purpose Questionnaire!

Circle the number that most closely represents you and your work. Check your total score below to see if YOU are a 21st century worker and thinker: self-aware, internally referenced, proactive, and responsible to the greater good of the world.

	MOST OFTEN	HALF THE TIME	RARELY
1. I think & act from the future of choice—not the past.	3	2	1
2. I know & leverage my unique skills & talents in the marketplace.	3	2	1
3. I act & work from a sense of greater good.	3	2	1
4. I am self-confident, self-responsible & self-managed.	3	2	1
5. I am a lifelong learner, always growing.	3	2	1
6. I'm passionate about my work purpose.	3	2	1
7. I am entrepreneurial in nature & act on new ideas.	3	2	1
8. I'm acting on "changing the way I change."	3	2	1
9. I work well in chaos & the unknown.	3	2	1
10. I'm a risk-taker, not resigned to 'business as usual.'	3	2	1
11. I see the future as bright with numerous possibilities.	3	2	1
12. I am at peace with myself & my work.	3	2	1

If You Scored 12-21...	If You Scored 22-27...	If You Scored 28-36...
This book is for you. Take the time necessary, and you will gain a renewed sense of self.	*You are straddling the fence between the past and the future. This process will ground you in the present.*	*You're a 21st Century worker and thinker. You are creating a new, enlightened way to work. This process will expand your effort.*

B. Success Is a Collective Effort – Supporting Each Other

Your success is a collective effort. You aren't meant to do this work alone—in fact, you can't. This work is best done in conjunction with others. We are in a time of collective effort and reward. We can thrive as a community of purposeful individuals. This is the only way true change will happen in the larger world of work.

The model for this is about "inter-independence" where you are firmly yourself in relationship to many others. You don't lose yourself in others nor sell your soul to someone else's dream. You are always a fully functioning human being, living and working with many others, not sacrificing any aspect of yourself along the way. You can benefit by the many gifts of others—utilizing their purpose in conjunction with yours. We need relationships and work arrangements that feed the souls of everyone involved.

> *I must give credit where credit is due. The idea of an inter-independent model for life and work was coined by my friend Ishwar. He was a very wise man in so many ways. I would like to propose a challenge to collectively create this inter-independent work and life model and to do this in his name and in the name of many others who have come before us. We are blessed today by the work of many enlightened, courageous souls who have sown many seeds. At some level they are with us and will guide us as we turn our purpose into thriving businesses.*

Some questions to consider based on this section:

1. Who are the various and best types of individuals to be part of your support system?

2. When are you going to contact and meet with them?

3. Who are the business partners and where are the alliances that are needed to create a larger whole and to be a force to be reckoned with?

4. What are the business groups that would be most aligned with your vision and mission? What do you need to do to become active and known within these groups?

5. What do you need to do to become YOUR best supporter?

We would also like to support you. Hopefully you have felt my support as you have progressed through this book. I have been with you, and I will continue to be there for you. Do take a minute to consider the following ways to say connected and continue to evolve.

1. As mentioned at the beginning of the book, you can sign up for our free monthly email newsletter, "The Evolution of Work," by going to our web site at www.internationalpurpose.com.

2. You can join us on Facebook or LinkedIn®.

3. Our Virtual Book Workshop is facilitated over the phone/on-line. It will provide you with a forum to interact with other readers and myself, to ask questions, as well as to receive encouragement and support as you work through the Seven Evolutionary Tools. See the web site for dates/times and investment.

4. You can become a member of a Purposeful Business Tele-Circle. These sessions are tailored to entrepreneurs and small business owners wanting to excel to the next level of their business by utilizing the Seven Evolutionary Tools. We meet by phone/on-line. Go to our web site for dates/times and investment.

C. It's Time to Celebrate

It's time to celebrate and thank all of you who have participated in this process. You deserve much praise and many well wishes. I'm sure, as with myself, this process has surfaced many emotions. Expressing all emotions is key to this endeavor, as we are true to ourselves in creating new work. And now is the time for JOY!

So how might you celebrate? There are so many ways:

1. A party of supporters, new and old, might be called for;
2. Maybe treating yourself to a spa for a day or more;
3. Creating a retreat for yourself to relax and regroup either in your backyard or at a retreat center;
4. Just some time with friends to open champagne and toast a well-done effort.

Whatever it is you do, do it with gusto. Have loads of fun with lots of laughter, and trust that you have done good work.

With lots of love—Purpose well done!
Patricia

ACKNOWLEDGMENTS

I am grateful to many for their assistance in the writing of this book. First and foremost, I would like to thank my many clients who have taken this journey with me. You are brave souls indeed and on the forefront of enlightened work in the world. I have learned much from you and will continue to do so.

I would like to thank everyone who has played a part in reading and editing the text and in contributing to International Purpose. This list starts with Diane, my sister, who has worked with me for over 15 years in many capacities and who is a backbone for the business; Karen and Deirdre are next on the list for first being good listeners and then always providing the input needed; Denise edited the book from front to back, tightening up the loose ends; Mary's eye caught errors I never saw; and Doug's beautiful work of art graces the cover.

Many thanks go to Mike, whose support I've had since the inception of International Purpose and who was truly a partner in the publishing process.

I would like to also thank my many friends and family members who have been cheerleaders along the way. Your belief in me was and is very important.

Last but not least, I would like to thank the powers that be for providing me with wisdom and guidance along the way. We were co-creators, and we did it!

THANK YOU'S

The following are clients/colleagues who contributed to the book through their own words and stories. I want to thank them for their part in making the world of work a better place.

Christine Beregi
Poet, Hospice Chaplain
cberegi@verizon.net
Pittsburgh, PA

Karen Gaskins-Jones
JLH Associates
www.jlhassociates.com
jlhassoc.jlhassoc@verizon.net
Upper Marlboro, MD

Maja Härri
Vertriebsoptimierung –
Coaching – Potentialanalyse
www.maja-haerri.de
kontakt@maja-haerri.de
Frankfurt, Germany

Pam Hawley
pjhawley@comcast.net
Pittsburgh, PA

Denice R. Hinden, PhD, ACC
Managance Consulting &
Coaching
www.managance.com
drhinden@managance.com
Silver Spring, MD

Bev Hitchins
ALIGN, A Unique and Integrative
Approach to Clutter and Balance
www.alignyourlife.net
bev@alignyourlife.net
Alexandria, VA

Dave Jackley
Director of Consulting
Seegrid Corporation
www.seegrid.com
djackley@seegrid.com
Djackley@verizon.net
Pittsburgh, PA

Vernestine Laughinghouse
Absolute Organizing Solutions
www.absouluteorg.com
aos@absouluteorg.com
Washington, DC

Teri Lim
Teri0920@earthlink.net
Los Angeles, CA

Ryta Mirisciotti
The Naked Grape
www.nakedgrape.net
ryta@nakedgrape.net
Sewickley, PA

Cynthia Moore MS, RD, CDE
Hygeia Well Being Center
cynhygeia@aol.com
Charlottesville, VA

Douglas G. Nelson
Artist
www.douglasgnelson.com
Ligonier, PA

Linda Rivero
lrivero@ganew-connect.com
Global Action Network of
Entrepreneurial Women
www.ganew-connect.com
Women Travel for Peace
www.womentravelforpeace.org
Peace Through Travel
www.peacethroughtravel.net
Washington, D.C. Metro

Mary Rossi
cabrinicreations@aol.com
Pittsburgh, PA

Michael Smith
TeraTech
www.teratech.com,
michael@teratech.com
Rockville, MD

BIBLIOGRAPHY

Aburdene, Patricia. *Megatrends 2010: The Rise of Conscious Capitalism.* Charlottesville: Hampton Roads Publishing, 2007.

Ambrose, Delorese, Ed.D. *Making Peace with Your Work: An Invitation to Find Meaning in the Madness.* Andover, MN: Expert Publishing, 2006.

Ambrose, Delorese, Ed.D. *Leadership: The Journey Inward,* 3rd Edition. Dubuque, Iowa: Kendall/Hunt Publishers, 2003.

Block, Peter. *Community: The Structure of Belonging.* San Francisco: Berrett-Koehler, 2008.

Block, Peter. *The Answer to How Is Yes: Acting on What Matters.* San Francisco: Berrett-Koehler, 2001.

Brattina, Anita F. *Diary of a Small Business Owner: A Personal Account of How I Built a Profitable Business.* Amacom, 1995.

Branden, Nathaniel. *The Art of Living Consciously: The Power of Awareness to Transform Everyday Life.* Simon & Schuster, 1997.

Branden, Nathaniel. *Six Pillars of Self-Esteem.* Bantam, 1995.

Byrne, Rhonda. *The Secret.* Atria Books, 2006.

Dalai Lama, His Holiness with Howard Cutler, M.D. *The Art of Happiness.* Riverhead Books, 1998.

Davis, Melinda. *The New Culture of Desire: 5 Radical New Strategies That Will Change Your Business and Your Life.* The Free Press, 2002.

Dr. Seuss. *Oh, The Places You'll Go!* New York: Random House, 1990.

Dyer, Wayne W. *The Shift: Taking Your Life from Ambition to Meaning.* Hay House, Inc., 2010.

Florida, Richard. *The Rise of the Creative Class.* Basic Books, 2004.

Fox, Matthew. *The Reinvention of Work: A New Vision of Livelihood for Our Time.* HarperSanFrancisco, 1994.

Fuller, R. Buckminster. *Operating Manual for Spaceship Earth.* Aeonian Press, Inc., 1976.

Goleman, Daniel and Cary Cherniss, edited for the Consortium for Research on Emotional Intelligence in Organizations. *The Emotionally Intelligent Workplace.* San Francisco: Jossey-Bass, 2001.

Hafiz, The Great Sufi Master. *The Gift.* Penguin Compass, 1999.

Hanh, Thich Nhat. *Peace In Every Step: The Path of Mindfulness in Everyday Life.* Bantam Books, 1992.

Helgesen, Sally. *Thriving in 24/7: Six Strategies for Taming the New World of Work.* New York: The Free Press, 2001.

Helgesen, Sally. *The Female Advantage: Women's Ways of Leadership.* New York: Doubleday Currency; 1990.

Hock, Dee. *Birth of the Chaordic Age.* Berrett-Koehler, 1999.

Houston, Jean. *Jump Time: Shaping Your Future in a World of Radical Change.* Tarcher, 2000.

Houston, Jean. *A Passion for the Possible: A Guide to Realizing Your True Potential.* Harper Collins, 1997.

Hubbard, Barbara Marx. *Conscious Evolution: Awakening the Power of Our Social Potential.* New World Library, 1998.

Kabat-Zinn, Jon. *Coming to Our Senses: Healing Ourselves and the World Through Mindfulness.* New York: Hyperion, 2005.

Katie, Byron. *Loving What Is: Four Questions That Can Change Your Life.* Harmony Books, 2002.

L'Engle, Madeleine. *A Wrinkle in Time.* New York: Farrar, Straus and Giroux, 1962.

Levoy, Gregg. *Callings: Finding and Following an Authentic Life.* Three Rivers Press, 1999.

Maurer, Rick. *Why Don't You Want What I Want? How to Win Support for Your Ideas without Hard Sell, Manipulation, or Power Plays.* Austin: Bard Press, 2002.

Maurer, Rick. *Beyond the Wall of Resistance: Unconventional Strategies that Build Support for Change.* Austin: Bard Press, 1996.

Percy, Ian. *Going Deep in Life and Leadership.* Toronto: Macmillan Canada, 1997.

Peters, Tom. *Re-imagine! Business Excellence in a Disruptive Age.* Dorling Kindersley Limited, 2003.

Pink, Daniel H. *A Whole New Mind: Why Right-Brainers Will Rule the Future.* Riverhead Books, 2006.

Ray, Michael and Alan Rinzler, edited for The World Business Academy. *The New Paradigm in Business.* New York: Tarcher/Putnam, 1993.

Ray, Paul H., Ph.D. and Sherry Ruth Anderson, Ph.D. *The Cultural Creatives: How 50 Million People are Changing the World.* Harmony Books, 2000.

Rifkin, Jeremy. *The End of Work.* New York: Tarcher/Putnam, 1995.

Ruiz, Don Miguel. *The Mastery of Love: A Practical Guide to the Art of Relationship.* Amber-Allen Publishing, 1999.

Thomas, Katherine Woodard. *Calling in "The One": Seven Weeks to Attract the Love of Your Life.* New York: Three Rivers Press, 2004.

Tolle, Eckhart. *A New Earth: Awakening to Your Life's Purpose.* Plume, 2006.

Tutu, Desmond. *No Future Without Forgiveness.* New York: Image, 2000.

Wacker, Watts and Jim Taylor with Howard Means. *The Visionary's Handbook: Nine Paradoxes That will Shape the Future of Your Business.* Harper Business, 2001.

Wheatley, Margaret J. *Turning to One Another: Simple Conversations to Restore Hope to the Future.* Berrett-Koehler, 2002.

Wheatley, Margaret J. *Leadership and the New Science: Discovering Order in a Chaotic World.* Berrett-Koehler, 1999.

Whyte, David. *Crossing the Unknown Sea: Work as a Pilgrimage of Identity.* Riverhead Books, 2001.

ABOUT THE AUTHOR

Patricia DiVecchio, President and Chief Visionary Officer of International Purpose, has over 25 years of experience working with individuals, small businesses and organizations in their evolutionary process to higher levels of work purpose and potential. Through her dynamic Coaching and Purposeful Business Circles/Tele-Circles, Patricia helps individuals to identify and leverage their unique skills and talents, small businesses to evolve their work and organizations to align with people, profit and planet. Patricia holds an M.A. in Human Resource Development from George Washington University and a B.A. in Education from the University of Pittsburgh. She has spoken at international conferences, and her initiatives have taken her to Senegal, Germany and other worldwide forums.